GENERAL & SOCIAL
LETTER WRITING

In the same series

The Right Way To Write Your Own CV
When Do I Start?
"The Job's Yours!"

Uniform with this book

GENERAL & SOCIAL LETTER WRITING

A. G. Elliot

RIGHT WAY

CONTENTS

DEDICATION

To Jill

who probably wrote more of this book than I did!

INTRODUCTION

The basic principles of letter writing are the same for both business and personal correspondence, but in this book I have concentrated on the writing of *personal* letters.

To aid the reader, I have split the book into three sections. The first deals with many general aspects applicable to all kinds of personal letters.

The second section deals with what I have called "official" correspondence which a private individual would send to a business or institution. Examples range from letters of complaint through to those written when you apply for a job.

The third section deals with social letters to friends, relatives or acquaintances. Get well messages, sympathy and invitations are some of the subjects covered.

It may be some consolation to those who find difficulty, to know that even the experienced writer is often confronted with a problem and, like the beginner, finds himself staring at paper without a thought or a word to put on it. It is useless to sit and look at the paper for a long time, because your mind is apt to become over concentrated on its task; far better to drop the matter for a few hours or even a day or two and come back to it again, when ideas may flow more readily.

I also hope that in studying the relevant passages in this book you will find that the ideas required are stimulated.

PART ONE

HANDY HINTS
FOR LETTER WRITERS

1
CHOOSING YOUR MATERIALS

This chapter will give you an idea of the different stationery
materials available, and I have included some personal tips on
what you should use, and when.

Paper
The paper you use generally depends on individual taste and
the amount of money you wish to spend. There is a wide variety
of colours, sizes and qualities of paper from which to choose,
and you can also have your stationery personalised with your
name, address and other details if you wish. (See **Printed
Notepaper** overleaf.)

You should try to avoid using very thin or flimsy paper as
it looks cheap. However, when writing to friends abroad, it is
a good idea to use lightweight paper and envelopes, as these
cost much less to send than ordinary stationery, so you will get
more pages for your money! Air Mail pads and envelopes are
widely available, and special all-in-one Aerogrammes can be
bought from post offices.

It is always sensible to use a colour of paper which suits the occasion. For instance, you should not really use a bright electric blue or a sunshine yellow paper when sending a sympathy letter or if applying for a job! Paper and envelopes are available in many lovely pastel shades, and if you choose one of these you will not go far wrong.

Although many people use lined paper, I personally think that a letter written on plain paper always looks more attractive and professional. Many plain writing pads include a lined page for use as a backing sheet, to enable you to get your written lines straight, or you can easily make one up yourself.

If you are concerned about the environment, you may like to buy recycled paper and envelopes which are becoming more widely available.

For information on choosing copy paper, see **Keeping Copies Of Correspondence** on page 47.

Printed Notepaper

As mentioned earlier, it is possible to have your address specially printed on your notepaper in a wide variety of colours and styles, and there are many high street print shops which can do this for you.

Many people like their printed letterhead to include their name, address and telephone number. It is not really necessary to include your name, as it will appear at the bottom along with your signature; and its inclusion would also prevent other members of the family from using the headed notepaper.

I, personally, would include my telephone number on my printed paper, though some prefer to have the option of writing it on if need be.

Printed notepaper does, undoubtedly, look very attractive, but if you are considering it, my advice would be to keep the design simple, and the words large enough for it to be read easily.

Before going ahead with your printed notepaper, see also **Setting Out Your Official Letters** and **Setting Out Your Social Letters** on pages 42 and 81 respectively. Here you will find further advice on the information to include on your headed notepaper, together with ideas on layout.

Another useful and practical idea is to have your address printed on small, self-adhesive labels. These work out to be fairly cheap; you can have hundreds printed for quite a reasonable price. Again, print shops can do this for you, or they can be bought by direct mail. These are useful for all sorts of purposes – not only for use on letters and postcards, but for identification purposes too (for example, if you lend a book). If you want to use these labels I would advise you to include your name, too, as they will not be used solely for correspondence.

Envelopes

Like paper, envelopes are available in many different sizes, colours and qualities. If you are writing a letter on coloured paper, it always looks better if it is sent in a matching envelope, and that the envelope is big enough for the size of paper you are using. Nothing looks worse than a piece of paper which has been folded several times to make it fit into its envelope!

Many people use smaller envelopes for their personal correspondence, as against the oblong ones used in business, but it really doesn't matter what type is used so long as it is capable of carrying the letter to its destination. That said, however, I wouldn't generally use a cheap manilla envelope for personal letter writing. Nor would I use a cheap envelope, of any kind, for sending out invitations.

When sending air mail letters to friends overseas, it is always a good idea to use a special air mail envelope. That way, there is no chance of it being accidentally sent by sea, when it could take months to arrive.

At post offices you can buy special envelopes for sending letters inland, which have printed on them a first or second class postage mark. It could be useful to have a few of these in reserve in case you run out of stamps and cannot get to a post office.

Cards and Notelets

Many people like to send a special card where they can write a personal note inside, and there is an enormous choice of cards available which carry no printed message in them.

This idea is very similar to sending notelets, which are generally sold in packs of six or ten. They are usually smaller, and work out cheaper, than individual cards and are ideal for writing a short note to a friend.

Postcards
Apart from holiday postcards, this method of communication seems to have gone out of fashion, although postcards do save an envelope and also a little time.

Some people have their name and address printed in small print across the tops of postcards, or they will use a blank postcard with a small self-adhesive address label. (See page 11.)

For any brief message, a postcard is ideal, but obviously, it must never be used to convey confidential information.

Writing Materials
Here again, there is a very wide range from which to choose − ball-points, fine-liners, felt-tips, etc. − and many traditionalists still like to use the fountain pen. All these are available in many different coloured inks, so you don't have to stick to the usual black or blue. You could always match your ink to your paper colour, and one very effective combination I have seen is cream coloured paper with brown ink.

Another choice is to type your letters, and for those whose handwriting is not very legible this is ideal.

I always feel that when sending a letter to a business (the bank, for instance) it is better typed, as important information is less likely to be misread, and a typed letter gives a greater feeling of professionalism.

It is often felt that typed personal letters appear less friendly, and I tend to agree. However, for those who are fast typists, it is much quicker to type a letter than to write it, and for long letters to friends, typing would be acceptable. In this case, I would be inclined to make an apology or a joke about the letter being typed, so as to avoid offending anyone.

It should really go without saying that writing letters or addressing envelopes with a pencil is not acceptable. Not only does it look bad, but there is a danger that it could become rubbed out or faded.

If for any reason you *have* to use a pencil because nothing else is available, I would always advise you to apologise for it.

There are still many people who would think it very bad taste to receive a letter written in pencil!

2

PUNCTUATION AND GRAMMAR

"Punctuation" is a word which frightens a great many people unnecessarily. Those who paid close attention to it at school may have no fears, but for the rest of us it is sometimes worrying. And that, I believe, is the worst feature of it; over-anxiety can lead us to make annoying little mistakes which we normally wouldn't make.

Most of us have a basic grasp of punctuation, but it is worth reminding ourselves of just what it means and when it should be used.

The first things to remember are, I think, the punctuation marks – the comma, the semi-colon, the colon, the full stop, the question mark, the exclamation mark, inverted commas, the apostrophe, the hyphen, brackets, and the dash.

Although this seems like a long list, many of these punctuation marks are not always used in general and social letter writing.

The Comma (,)

Always think of the comma as the smallest stop. In other words, put it in where, if you were speaking, you would stop to breathe, or where there is a natural pause.

Many people think that a comma is unnecessary before the words "and" and "but". Generally this is true but in some instances a comma before these words can make the sentence clearer or more easily read.

If commas are left out, a sentence can read wrongly and might be misunderstood, however, for this very same reason many lawyers leave out all commas when drawing up legal documents!

Basically, commas are used at the ends of phrases or where

you would pause to take a breath. Therefore, provided you don't insert one in the middle of a clause, you can't go wrong. The main thing to remember is to put them in your sentences when a slight break is required.

Below is an example to illustrate the misuse and use of the comma:

Karen and James have decided to go down to the coast for the weekend so they've booked their hotel checked the car and had a look at the map to find the best route.

Although it can be understood, see how much easier this sentence reads when it has a few commas in it:

Karen and James have decided to go down to the coast for the weekend, so they've booked their hotel, checked the car, and had a look at the map to find the best route.

The Semi-colon (;)

The semi-colon is used when you need a slightly longer pause than that which you would get with a comma. A semi-colon very often forms a substitute for a full stop, to avoid starting too many new sentences. Notice that the ideas after a semi-colon have to relate in some way to those immediately before it. Below is an example of how to use the semi-colon:

Karen and James enjoyed their trip to the coast at the weekend; the weather was beautiful and they spent much of their time water-skiing.

The Colon (:)

The colon is generally used before a list, or as an indication that something is to follow, for example:

The following people were elected to the committee:

> Natalie Hardwick
> Sarah Hamilton
> Simon Phillips
> Richard Castleton.

The Full Stop (.)

The full stop is used where a definite break is necessary and where the sentence is complete. If no full stops were inserted in a piece of writing, it would be almost impossible to read. For examples, have a look at the sentences in this book.

The Exclamation Mark (!)
This is mainly used to express surprise, emphasis, sarcasm or humour, as in the following examples:

The cat's had *eight* kittens!
Peter told the dog to STAY!
Why on earth did you think I'd want *that*!
We're having a new bathroom put in, so the place is like a building site at the moment!

The Question Mark?
This follows a direct question where an answer is required, as well as a rhetorical question, which is a statement in the form of a question. Examples of this are given below:

May I come in? (Direct)
What sort of a remark do you call *that*? (Rhetorical; used for effect.)

Inverted Commas (" ")
These are often referred to as quotes. They are generally used to enclose an extract or quotation, or when recalling what someone has said. For example:

"If music be the food of love, play on."
(Quotation from *Twelfth Night* by William Shakespeare.)
"The football's started", shouted Paul.

The Apostrophe (')
This can indicate that a letter has been left out of a word; for instance if you are changing "have not" to "haven't" it shows that the "o" has been omitted.

Many people are unsure of how to use the apostrophe with the word "it". The general rule is that if you can't substitute "it is", or "it has", when you read your sentence, it should be "its" (i.e. no apostrophe). For example, "the dog scratched its leg" (correct; you could not put in "it is"). However, if you say, "it's the only one we have", this would be correct because you could easily substitute "it is" in the place of "it's; or "it's been raining today" — correct again, "it has" could be inserted.

The apostrophe is also used when denoting ownership, to make a shorter and better phrase as, for example, "the woman's coat", rather than "the coat of the woman". In the same way, it is used with plural words, in particular when, to form the plural, an "s", or sometimes "es" is just tacked on to the singular word; for example, "boys" (more than one boy). So if you wanted to say "the socks of several boys" you would write "the boys' socks".

However when using a *collective* word (different from a plural word but which still suggests more than one person or thing), like "children" or "people", the apostrophe goes *before* the "s"; i.e. "the children's pony", or "the people's cars".

An increasingly common error is the redundant or unnecessary apostrophe, when an apostrophe is inserted into a perfectly ordinary plural word. At one time, this was confined to greengrocers' notices (Apple's, Banana's, Avocado's, etc.), but it is now often seen even in newspapers and magazines. Needless to say, it is quite wrong, and this error needs to be stamped out.

Brackets ( )
These are used where something is put into a sentence, usually to clarify the meaning, but which has no direct effect on the sense of the sentence. For example:

The boys (there were four of them) stood at the bus stop.

Alternatively, commas could be used in the place of the brackets.

Dashes and Hyphens (–)
When printed, dashes are usually longer than hyphens; and these two punctuation marks have quite different meanings.

Dashes are often used instead of commas or semi-colons. The best explanation of a dash is to give a couple of examples.

The couple — still covered in confetti — went off on honeymoon.

Sorry I've taken so long to reply – I can't believe it's October already!

The hyphen can be used when two words would read better as one, as in:

self-sufficient
flip-flops
second-hand
non-starter.

OPEN PUNCTUATION

This refers to the omission of commas and full stops in the salutation, complimentary closing (see page 44) and addresses of your letters. It is common in typewritten material, especially business letters, because it saves time in the typing.

In hand-written letters, although many people leave out the comma at the end of each line of the address, it is still usual to put the full stop after "Mr./Mrs.", etc., and to include the comma after "Dear *name*,". In the same way, when you finish a hand-written letter, you would always include the comma after "Yours sincerely,".

The Post Office request the use of open punctuation on envelopes.

In this book, I have used open punctuation for official letters, as, for example, in Chapter 7. Where a letter would obviously be a hand-written one, I have included commas and full stops where appropriate.

GRAMMAR

The trouble with grammar, as with punctuation, is that many people tend to worry too much about it. Grammar should be learned almost unconsciously. If you listen to and read well-spoken and written English, you will acquire the right habits and will rarely find yourself going wrong. However, there are a few rules which can be remembered as a guide.

(a) Ask yourself what is wrong with the words "for you and I", and the answer is that it should be "for you and me". This you can prove by filling in the missing word "for", making the full phrase "for you and (for) me". You will then see that the first phrase "for you and I" could not be correct.

(b)   Always be sure that a sentence is complete; that is, complete with subject (a noun or pronoun) and verb. Here is an example, "She went to the door to open it. But did not try." The first sentence is complete, the second is not because it has no subject. It should read, "But she did not try."

Here is an example of a sentence which is incomplete because the subject and verb have been omitted: "Standing on the pavement with the dog". If, before the word "standing", you put the words "I was", the sentence would be complete.

(c)   It is usually better not to end a sentence with a preposition. An example of this is the following sentence: "This is the letter which I've been waiting for". The sentence should read: "This is the letter for which I've been waiting".

(d)   "And" and "but" are words which should, as far as possible, be kept away from the beginnings of sentences. However, they are sometimes used there on purpose, for emphasis.

(e)   Another difficulty that arises is the use of "either -- or" and "neither -- nor". So often you read sentences such as this: "She looked, but he was neither in the garage or the garden." Here, confusion has led to the mixing of the positive and negative sentence. In this — the negative sentence — it should read: "She looked, but he was neither in the garage *nor* the garden."

The positive example would be as follows: "She thought he must be in either the garage or the garden."

(f)   *Split infinitive:* This is a very common fault not least because, more often than not, it sounds more correct the *wrong* way than the right! An example of a split infinitive is: "I would like you to urgently send your new catalogue." Here, "urgently" has been inserted between the sign of the infinitive, "to", and its verb, "send". The sentence should read: "I would like you to send urgently your new catalogue." OR: "I would like you urgently to send your new catalogue."

The rule here is never to split the word "to" from its verb.

Although it is better to try and get your grammar and punctuation correct in anything you write, remember that they are not the most important things in your letters.

What matters is what your letters say; and what they say results from the amount of thought and consideration that you have given to them.

This is particularly the case when writing to friends, who will be delighted that you have taken the trouble to write at all!

Write as if you are speaking your thoughts aloud; pack your letters with interesting news and information that your readers will enjoy. Worry more about the content of your letter than about the grammar or punctuation, and you will not go far wrong.

3

WRITING STYLE AND LETTER LAYOUT

WRITING STYLE

There is quite a lot of confusion about style. Many people are not sure what it means. I think a good definition of it would be that it is the manner in which you, as an individual, express your thoughts. Therefore, don't let style be a bugbear to you as it is to many people. I will go further and say that if you have good subject matter, your style will largely look after itself. What might be called the "niceties of style" can, of course, be developed, and are acquired perhaps by the wide reading of experienced authors, noting how, in practice, they express their ideas and thoughts.

The main thing to remember about style is to keep your writing simple and straightforward, because anything which is too involved and complicated is bad writing.

Here is an example of muddled style.

Dear Mark,

I have just seen Roger Langton about the forthcoming meeting and he has made various different suggestions about the place and time. We do not know whether the meeting will be large or small but it would probably be best to hold it in the Buckingham Room and Roger thinks the time should be 8.30 not 7.30 otherwise there might not be room for everyone.

Yours

You can see at a glance that the writer of the above paragraph did not have clearly in mind what he wanted to convey. Let us analyse sentence by sentence. His first sentence is quite clear, but his second is very muddled; it should read:

We don't know how big the meeting will be, so it will probably be best to hold it in the Buckingham Room, otherwise there might not be enough room for everyone. Roger also thinks that it would be better if we held the meeting at 8.30 instead of 7.30.

This simple example shows the advantage of the short sentence for clarity.

Another important point is to avoid using superfluous words and adjectives. In speaking, it is sometimes necessary to repeat what has been said and to use adjectives such as "very" for effect and emphasis, but in writing it is wise to avoid any repetition as far as possible. The reason for this is simply that the written word can be read over again if necessary.

One of the greatest faults of a letter writer is he who pumps one adjective from beginning to end — wonderful day — wonderful food — wonderful beaches. Imagine how irritating a letter of this kind can become. (It's irritating enough if people do this when they're speaking!)

We can all remember being taught at school not to use the same adjective twice in the same sentence or even on the same page, but I feel that this is going a bit too far. Quite often it is not worth changing a word because it has been used a few lines above. Indeed, some writers use deliberate repetition of a word for emphasis, as I have done in the previous paragraph!

I think it is much more important to avoid repetition of information in a sequence of similar words. If you wish to emphasise something it may be necessary to go over the ground again. But use different arguments and try to present the question from a different angle. So, you must not only keep out superfluous words, but, more important, superfluous information. In a social letter this does not mean you should leave out detail, provided it is of interest.

Style alone, in the form of a lot of words correctly put together, can be boring in the extreme. In short — matter, rather than manner, is what matters. (Note repetition of the word matter for effect!)

Have something to write and there will be no need to worry about how to write it. Style comes easily to those who have interesting facts to convey. Qualities such as subtlety of method, lightness in style, and humorous ways of writing can soon be achieved by a little thought and practice, and by studying how they are accomplished by others.

But do not *try* to develop style. Your own is probably far better than any which you may copy. Absorb ideas and layouts from well written books and the classics if you like, but don't consciously imitate them. After all, however badly you may write, the recipient is more interested in you than in your attempts to impress by a style which is not part of you.

There is so much to do these days — and so little time — that the day of the many-paged letter is almost over, except for those who have much time and little to do, or who have friends or relatives who live overseas.

You therefore need a crisp and compact style. One way to help you accomplish this is to study the short leader articles in the popular daily papers, and learn how they achieve effect and grab the interest.

Another method of improving your style is to read lots of the letters which appear in the daily press. These are usually of an extremely high standard, otherwise they would not get printed.

You could also try observing the styles — both good and bad — of letters which are sent to you. This way you will quickly see where you may, in your own writing, be going wrong, or indeed where your correspondents haven't got something quite right!

LETTER LAYOUT

Most of us have received letters which began at the far left hand corner of the page, and filled the whole paper without any margins and with very few paragraphs. Not only is the effect of such a letter crowded and messy, but it also makes the contents difficult to understand and follow.

The aim of letter writing is to convey information, and the whole purpose of layout, or construction, is to make the information easily followed by the reader and pleasing to see.

It is, therefore, advisable always to leave about 2cm of margin all round the letter. (This could be reduced to about 1cm if you were using small-sized paper; but no less.) In all letters you should leave enough space between the lines to make them easily read.

There is, however, a bit more to it than this, and for example, in "official" letters or in social letters where you want to stress certain information, there are various hints which you can use.

If you have quite a lot of information to convey, it is a good idea to set it out in numbered points. That way, the reader will more easily be able either to act on the information given, or, if the numbered points are queries, answer each one in turn. Nothing is more annoying than having information or queries overlooked.

This would only really apply to "official" letters, as the majority of letters to friends carry information of a social nature. However, if you are arranging a meeting, or something equally important, it is sensible to set this information out in a paragraph of its own.

Paragraphing And Setting Out
I have already described, in Chapter 2, the construction of the sentence.

Generally speaking, a paragraph is composed of several sentences dealing with the same subject. This, however, must be qualified, because one could write a ten page letter composed of sentences dealing with the same subject. As you can see, one paragraph of such a length would make a letter extremely difficult to follow as well as giving the reader no pause or break. It is, therefore, often a matter of common sense where you break your paragraphs.

As a general guide, you should bear in mind that a paragraph should preferably be not more than about fifteen or at the most twenty lines, with an average of perhaps eight to ten lines as an ideal paragraph length. A letter composed of these average paragraphs is easy to read and follow, but this is only a guide, and there is no fixed rule. A paragraph can vary from between one line to pages in length.

You must, however, avoid starting new paragraphs just for

the sake of it. Equally, you should avoid running two different subjects together because one paragraph may be a little short. In other words, don't be afraid of short paragraphs where necessary. Here is a letter written in paragraphs to show their uses.

Dear Jonathan,

I was so pleased to hear from you, and I'm glad you all had a good holiday. Did you get caught in the traffic on the way back?

Life here has been quite busy lately. We had our annual garden fête last Saturday, with a Fancy Dress Dance at the village hall in the evening.

The weather was lovely for the fête, and we had a good variety of stalls. I was on the plant stall, and I took a lot of cuttings from my greenhouse plants. Old Mr. Barker, my next door neighbour, is also a keen gardener and he gave me a lot of plants, so I had a good show.

The Fancy Dress Dance in the evening was absolutely hilarious! Our friend, Peter, went as Tarzan! And I don't mind telling you that his fake-fur leopard skin loin cloth proved to be the life and soul of the party! I wondered if he might start swinging from the village hall rafters after he'd had a few, but he didn't; he just kept beating his chest and doing the "Aargh..." Tarzan call, and eating the bunch of bananas he'd brought!

Sarah went as Cinderella (she looked smashing), and Jeff and I went as the Ugly Sisters! We didn't look quite so smashing — especially after one of Jeff's 'balloons' burst when he was dancing with the vicar's wife!

It really was a great evening, and a good time was had by all. We're now back to normal. (Well almost, apart from Ben who went as the Incredible Hulk and is still trying to wash off the green colouring ... but that's another story!)

My job has been taking me all over the country lately; in fact, I'll be down your way next Thursday. Would it be O.K. to pop in for a cup of tea? I'll give you a call when I'm in your area to see what would be a good time. I expect I'll be finished by about 4 p.m.

Anyway, must finish now so I can cut the hedge before the daylight goes. Hope to see you all next week.

'Bye for now ...

The above shows the use of paragraphs of different length, and although most of the letter is about two subjects — the garden fête and the dance — it illustrates the way in which the different aspects can be separated so that each has its own paragraph.

Note: It is usual in the hand-written letter to indent each paragraph. That means that the first word of a new paragraph is moved in to the right by three or four letter spaces, as in the letter above.

By typesetting convention, the setting out of the remaining letters in this book do not follow this rule. However, it is worth remembering to indent your paragraphs when writing letters by hand, because it makes each paragraph easier to distinguish from the one before.

In typewritten letters indenting can be used, although it is more common nowadays to adopt the fully blocked style without indentation, instead, leaving an extra line between paragraphs. The rest of the letters in this book follow this style.

4

FORMS OF ADDRESS AND SUBSCRIPTION

Fortunately, there is less formality in addressing people of different rank nowadays than there used to be, and much less importance is attached to any minor slip. Nevertheless, it is still courteous to address such people correctly, so I have included the following list. (Open punctuation – see page 18 – is used.)

UNTITLED PEOPLE

MAN	Dear Sir or Dear Mr (Mr on envelope)
WOMAN	Dear Madam or Dear Mrs or Dear Miss or Dear Ms (Mrs, Miss or Ms on envelope)
TWO OR MORE MARRIED WOMEN	Dear Mesdames (Mesdames *name* and *name* on envelope)
TWO OR MORE SPINSTERS	Dear Misses (The Misses *name* on envelope)
Two business women can be addressed simply in the salutation of a letter as	Dear Ladies

HUSBAND AND WIFE   Dear Mr and Mrs (no
                         initials or degrees, etc.)
                         (Mr and Mrs on envelope)
BOYS UNDER 14   Dear *Christian name*
                         (Master and *Christian name*
                         on envelope)

The abbreviation for any degrees or qualifications a person may use are put after the name on the envelope, e.g. Mr Peter Jameson, BSc.

You may still find "Esquire" or "Esq". used on the envelope when addressing a man who owns land.

PERSONS OF RANK

	On envelope	*To open and close the letter*
DUKE	His Grace the Duke of	My Lord Duke or Your Grace (refer to as "Your Grace") (I remain, my Lord Duke)
DUCHESS	Her Grace the Duchess of	Madam ("Your Grace") (I remain, Madam)
MARQUIS	The Most Hon. the Marquis of	My Lord Marquis ("Your Lordship") (I remain, my Lord Marquis)
MARCHIONESS	The Most Hon. the Marchioness of	Madam ("Your Ladyship") (I remain, Madam)
EARL	The Right Hon. the Earl of	My Lord ("Your Lordship") (I remain, my Lord)

COUNTESS	The Right Hon. the Countess of	Madam ("Your Ladyship") (I remain, Madam)
VISCOUNT	The Right Hon. the (Lord) Viscount	My Lord ("Your Lordship") (I remain, my Lord)
VISCOUNTESS	The Right Hon. the Viscountess, or, The Viscountess	Madam ("Your Ladyship") (I remain, Madam)
BARON	The Right Hon. Lord, or, The Lord	My Lord ("Your Lordship") (I remain, my Lord)
BARONESS	The Right Hon. the, or, The Baroness	My Lady ("Your Ladyship") (I remain, my Lady)
BARONET	Sir James Milwall Bart. or Bt.	Sir (I am, Sir)
BARONET'S WIFE	Lady Milwall	Madam ("Your Ladyship") (I am, Madam)
KNIGHT	Sir John Newell	Sir (between friends, Dear Sir John) (I am, Sir)
KNIGHT'S WIFE	Lady Newell	Madam (between friends, Dear Lady XX) (I am, Madam)
ARCHBISHOP (English)	His Grace the Lord Archbishop of	My Lord Archbishop ("Your Grace")
BISHOP	The Right Rev. the Lord Bishop of,	My Lord Bishop ("Your Lordship")

	or, The Lord Bishop of	
DEAN	The Very Rev. the Dean of	Very Rev. Sir (formal); Mr Dean
CLERGY	The Rev. William Lockwood (if a Doctor of Divinity, add DD)	Rev. Sir (formal) Dear Sir, Dear Mr, or, if a DD, Dear Dr
JUDGE	The Hon. Mr Justice	Sir
PRIVY COUNCILLORS	The Right Hon. Michael Quarterly MP	Sir (Yours faithfully)
MEMBERS OF PARLIAMENT	Mr David Jones MP Sir Roy Farjeon MP	Sir or Dear Sir (Yours faithfully)
DOCTOR	Dr Peter Ransome	Dear Sir, or, Dear Dr
SURGEON	Mr Philip Palmer FRCS	Dear Sir, or Dear Mr

Commissioned officers of HM Forces are addressed by rank, together with decorations, if any. For Naval officers, add RN. Army officers may have their arm of Service added, e.g. RA, RE.

5

DANGERS OF THE WRITTEN WORD

Libel, Slander And Defamation Of Character

The wit who said, "Do right and fear no man; don't write and fear no woman", exaggerated. However, it is true that many letters are written which in law undoubtedly provide grounds for libel, defamation of character or even breach of promise but of which, for a variety of reasons, nothing more is heard.

The word "libel" means any malicious or defamatory piece of writing, art, recording or broadcast, and must be avoided at all costs, unless done under privilege. ("Slander" has basically the same meaning, but applies to the spoken word.)

It is also widely believed that the truth is not libellous nor slanderous, but this is not necessarily so. Indeed, the truth can possibly be more dangerous than fiction.

Let us imagine that my next door neighbour had assaulted somebody twenty years ago and had received a term of imprisonment; in other words he had committed a crime and paid the legal penalty. It would be the truth if I should inform others in the neighbourhood that this man who had recently become my neighbour was an ex-convict, but you can see how unfair it would be to him, because the conviction was so long ago that it is "spent". He could, in my opinion rightly, take action against me.

Libel, being written, is more punishable in law than slander, because of the permanency of the written word.

The letter beginning "I am writing to tell you what I think of you", and continuing to inform the recipient what you think of him, can be libellous. Although addressed to the individual and not "published", the fact that it has been written and sent is in itself publication. However, there are instances where statements can be made quite legally, if done in the proper manner.

Perhaps the most common example is a reference as to character or integrity; if something disparaging has to be said, provided it is done in good faith and without malice, and what is said is true and headed "Private & Confidential", much can be written which would otherwise be actionable. (See also page 72.) It is, of course, essential for the envelope containing the information to be properly sealed and also marked "Private & Confidential", and carefully addressed to the correct recipient.

Sending A 'Threatening' Letter

Another potential danger is that some people may, in the heat of the moment, make a written threat without realising the possible legal consequences. The law takes an extremely serious view of anything of this nature. For example, someone in a fit of anger may write:

If you don't stop parking your car across my driveway, I'll smash it to bits and dump it in your front garden.

As you can imagine, it is extremely unwise to write anything of this kind, where you are basically saying that you will take the law into your own hands. There are legal processes which exist to resolve such situations.

If such a letter has to be sent, it could be written in a legal way, for example:

Private and Confidential (envelope the same)
For several days now you have been parking your car across my driveway so that I am unable to get into my garage. As I am sure you would not want me to refer the matter to my solicitor, will you please stop doing this immediately.

So long as you were sure, and had some evidence of the problem, there could be no danger in sending such a letter; although, depending on the seriousness of the situation, you may not need to mention your solicitor.

Receiving A Threatening Letter

If you receive a written threat that has obviously been written purely in the heat of the moment, probably your best solution would be just to ignore it.

However, if you receive a *serious* written threat you should consult a solicitor, or put the matter into the hands of the police. The difficulty of the latter procedure is that the police might insist on taking some action, against your wishes; whereas, normally, a solicitor will be guided by your instructions.

Blackmail

Blackmail is where money or some service is demanded under threat of exposure. It doesn't matter whether the information the sender threatens to expose is true or false; the law takes a very grave view of the blackmailer.

We are always seeing reports in the Press where prominent figures have been the subject of blackmail threats when their letters have fallen into the hands of unauthorised (and unscrupulous) people. This illustrates only too clearly how careful we should all be when writing anything of a confidential nature.

Chain Letters

At some time in our lives, almost every one of us will receive a chain letter. The concept behind them is to perpetuate the chain, by the recipient sending copies of the letter to others. Many also involve the sending of money.

Chain letters will normally be sent to you by someone you know. However, it is unlikely that you will know who originated the letter, as such letters can be in existence for many months, or even years.

Some chain letters can contain veiled threats, or are designed to intimidate the recipient into continuing the chain. These, however, seem to be few and far between, and most chain letters are no more than a nuisance.

What to do with them is up to you, but personally, I always throw any chain letters straight in the bin!

Pen Friends

Thousands of people make use of pen friend clubs which can

be found all over the world. In many cases, it is a way of making new friends from different countries and cultures. In most instances, the resulting friendships are innocent and genuine, and many pen friends, who may have been corresponding for years, do get the chance to meet.

There is, however, a danger that pen friend clubs could be joined by ill-intentioned people for unpleasant or perverted reasons, and one must always be aware of this fact if making arrangements to meet a pen friend — however long you have been writing to them.

The dangers of the written word with which we are mainly concerned, are more of a social nature than of a legal one. There is no question that letters can be the cause of family squabbles and of serious differences, sometimes tragic, between friends, purely owing to hasty action or misunderstandings.

The message of this short chapter is to advise the reader to be extremely careful in writing anything of a dangerous character, and to be careful that the phrasing of the letter is such that it cannot be misunderstood.

Letters should not be written in the heat of the moment, or, if they are, they should be laid aside and considered the next day. When something disagreeable has to be said to someone, or about someone, it is very much safer to do so verbally and in confidence.

It must be realised that between close friends much more can be written than could be sent to comparative strangers. It is largely a question of knowing to whom you are writing, but the need for care is always present. Think twice before you write once.

Copyright

Another pitfall which you could encounter (and of which you may not be aware) when you write is breach of copyright.

Whenever anything is spoken or written, it automatically becomes copyright. Even in a private letter one must not quote others without permission and acknowledgement of the source. That is the legal position but, of course, if you are quoting in a letter what your wife said when she sat on a pin ...

Well, that's different!

Again, it is normal practice to quote brief extracts, using inverted commas, from various printed sources, provided you are using them to explain some point, or confirm some view you hold. Give the source of the extract, especially if it is a long one.

Quoting from another source in a personal letter is quite different from doing so in material which is going to be published for the public. This cannot be done safely without permission. A good example of this type of letter would be one to The Editor of a newspaper, where permission to publish is taken as being granted. See page 79.

6

ADDRESSING ENVELOPES, SENDING YOUR LETTERS AND ANSWERING YOUR MAIL

ADDRESSING ENVELOPES

Included in this section is advice on the information you should put on your envelopes and the correct way to set it out.

Addressing an Envelope to a U.K. Address

When addressing an envelope to someone in the U.K., always try to put the postcode on a line on its own, and to make it the last line of the address. It must be clearly printed in capitals, with no punctuation, and it should not be underlined. Leave a small gap between the two halves of the code. If you do not have enough space to put the postcode on its own line, it is acceptable to put it alongside the county name, leaving a space of about 2cm between them. It is worth noting that if you are writing to the United Kingdom from abroad, the postcode should still be the last line of the address.

It is also preferable to put the main postal town, which must be written clearly in capitals, on its own line.

Where possible, you should try to include the name of the county, particularly if you are sending something to a town which has the same name as others located in different counties — like Ashford or Newport.

If your letter is going to someone who lives in a country village which has a larger post town, it is not necessary to put the words "Near" or "By" before the name of the post town. Nor should you any longer put the word "Local" if the letter is going to someone in your own area.

Below are two examples of how to write the types of addresses mentioned above. Note the use of capital letters and open punctuation in both.

Mrs Geraldine Steele	Mr P Jones
12 Viking Avenue	8 The Grove
Wishingbury	ST ALBANS
BRISTOL	Hertfordshire
Avon BS7 5PQ	UNITED KINGDOM
	AL10 9PP

The name and address of the recipient should be placed in the *bottom* half of the front of the envelope, slightly to the left hand side. One simple reason for this is that if you write the address too high up, you may not have enough room for the stamp(s). (How many of us have written the address too high on our small Christmas card envelopes, only to find that the name is partially covered by a lovely big Christmas stamp!) Another reason is that the name and/or address could become obliterated by the postmark if it is written too high up.

If you are writing to someone you think may have moved, it is a good idea to put the words "Please Forward" on the front of the envelope, in the top left hand corner, and to write on the flap on the reverse of the envelope, "If undelivered, please return to", then your name and address. This saves either the current occupants (who may not have a forwarding address), or the Post Office, opening your private mail to find out to whom they should return the letter. For the same reason, it is also sensible to include your address on the back of the envelope if you write to someone with whom you have not corresponded for a long time.

Addressing an Envelope to an Overseas Address
Much of the advice above also applies here, and again, you should always write the address in the bottom half of the front of the envelope, slightly to the left.

Any Air Mail stickers or other service instructions should be placed or written on the front of the envelope in the top left hand corner. As a general rule when writing overseas, I would always put on the reverse outside flap of the envelope "If undelivered please return to", followed by my name and address. Again, it saves having personal mail opened if it cannot be delivered for any reason.

Other countries have their own coding systems (called 'zip' codes in many places, such as the U.S.A. and Australia), which are similar to our postcodes, and these need to be clearly marked. However, when writing overseas from the United Kingdom, you should make the country of destination the last line of the address. Imagine how frustrating it would be if a letter bound for Kingston, Jamaica ended up in Kingston, Surrey!

Stamping Your Mail

The correct place for a stamp is on the front of the envelope in the top right hand corner. If possible, use only one stamp of the correct value. However, if you have to use more than one stamp, they should be placed side by side. Do not cover stamps with sticky tape as the Post Office need to be able to cancel them.

SENDING YOUR LETTERS

There are many ways in which you can send your mail within the U.K. and to overseas destinations, and it is not really possible to give details of them all in a book of this kind.

Apart from the obvious first and second class postal services, some others available are: Recorded Delivery, Registered Post and Special Delivery. It is worth bearing in mind that all these services will cost you – to a greater or lesser degree – more than if you sent your item by ordinary first class post; and that hardly anything is so annoying as to receive a letter by one of these means which contains information of little or no importance or urgency.

There is obviously a great deal to know about the various postal services available, and for more information I would suggest you ask at your local post office, or consult *The Post Office Guide*, a copy of which should be in the reference section of your local library.

ANSWERING YOUR MAIL

One would hardly imagine it necessary to write a section on answering a letter, but from long experience of replying to correspondence and having my letters answered, I regard this as one of the most important sections of the book.

The first rule about answering a letter is obviously to *ANSWER* it, and this is where so many people go wrong. Frequently in social letters and more often in official letters there may be three, six or more different matters for attention. What so often happens is that the reply covers a few of them, but the other points raised are just ignored, which is, to say the least, extremely exasperating for the recipient, who is expecting answers to *all* his queries.

The best way to reply to a letter which raises several points is to have it in front of you, and as you answer the various questions or matters raised you can draw a line through the relative part of the letter. In this way you can see at a glance when you have replied to everything.

It is not always easy, in this busy day and age, to reply to letters by return, but you should try to do so if possible − particularly when dealing with official correspondence (see next chapter). This is not just because replying by return gives a good impression, but because there is nothing easier than putting off the writing of a letter, and days of delay are liable to spread into months.

PART TWO

OFFICIAL LETTERS

7

STARTING AN OFFICIAL LETTER

Introduction

The term "official" in this book refers to all letters that are not of a social nature, and would usually mean a letter written to a business or institution, or on behalf of an official body. The content and construction of such letters is normally quite different from social correspondence, which is why each has been dealt with separately in this book.

There are many different businesses to which you may write – for example, your bank or building society, the electricity, gas, and telephone companies, or to your solicitor. You may also write letters on behalf of a local group, or contact a mail-order company requesting their latest catalogue. You might send letters to charities, the local council or to your M.P. The list is endless. Nevertheless, the layout is basically the same for all official letters.

Presentation

It is most important that these letters can be easily read and understood. I always try to type any official letters, as I feel they look more professional, but it is perfectly acceptable to hand-write them. However, when doing so, your handwriting should be as neat as possible. You can imagine the headaches it could cause if information in a letter of this kind were to be misread.

It is vital that your name and address are clearly written, particularly if you are expecting a reply from someone who doesn't know you or your address. A good example of this is when sending away for something by mail order. *You* know what your name is and where you live, but it can be a real puzzle for the company concerned when they try to work out where and to whom they should send the goods!

Setting Out Your Official Letters
The first things you should put on the letter are your address, the recipient's address, and the date. If you do not want to go to the expense of printed notepaper (see page 10), it is quite adequate to write neatly your full address at the top of the paper.

Advising you to put your address on a letter may seem obvious, but it is surprising how many people write away for goods and do not include a return address!

There is no real necessity to include your name at the top with the address, as it will be written at the bottom along with your signature. I would normally include my telephone number but many people leave it out of the printed part and only write it in if they need an urgent response to the letter.

On any official correspondence, you should always include the full name and address of the recipient. The reason is that, as it will appear on your copy of the letter (see **Keeping Copies of Correspondence** on page 47), you will then have an address (and usually a name) reference in case of further correspondence.

It is most important to put the date on all official letters as it could make quite a difference, for instance when renewing insurance. A dated letter is also useful if you are expecting a reply, as you can see at a glance how long it is since you sent the letter.

Opposite is an example of the way in which I normally begin my official letters. I place my address at the right hand margin, with the date below this. I then start writing/typing my recipient's name and address at the left hand margin on or just below the same line as the date.

27 Cherry Way
HORSHAM
East Sussex
RH14 4BT

Mr James Williams   *(the date)*
James Williams & Co Ltd
10 Eastfield Street
NEWCASTLE-UPON-TYNE
Tyne & Wear
NE6 7HY

The paragraphs of my letter are *blocked* at the left-hand margin,
i.e. they are not indented. Instead, I leave an extra line space
between them. You will notice that there is no punctuation in
either of the addresses, nor would there be in the date, the "Dear
Sir", or the "Yours faithfully". As explained on page 18, this
is described as *open punctuation*. There would, of course, be
punctuation in the body of the letter itself!

Note here, that the main postal towns are in capitals, and they
should always be on their own lines, if possible, as should the
postcodes. It is also useful to include the county name in any
address, as you will not always be writing to people from your
own locality who know where your town is situated.

If you wished, you could use the *fully blocked* style. With
this, you block *everything* at the left-hand margin, including your
own address and the date, as in the following:

(your address)

(the date)

(recipient's address)

This second way is a very simple way to set out a letter, but
it does take up a lot of space on the page.

You can also place your address and date information at the
top, in the centre, but I don't feel that this works very well for
letters to businesses and I, personally, would only use this style

of layout when writing a letter to a friend (see page 82).

Opening And Closing

These are the "Dear ..." and "Yours ..." parts of your letter. The first of these is the 'opening', and is technically known as the *salutation*. The correct name for the 'closing' line is the *complimentary closing*.

There are really only two basic ways to start and end a letter to a business, so it couldn't be more simple. When writing to a named individual, you finish "Yours sincerely"; when you don't know a specific name, the letter should end "Yours faithfully". The following are the opening and closing lines which would therefore be used in the same letter.

Opening	*Closing*
Dear Sir(s), or,	Yours faithfully
Dear Madam	
Dear Mr/Mrs/Miss/Ms Smith,	
or, Dear John	Yours sincerely

If starting a letter with "Dear John", you could end with *Yours truly,* though I feel that this is a little outdated now.

When writing to a company (rather than to an office holder at the company), you would start *Dear Sirs,* or perhaps *Dear Sir or Madam* and close with *Yours faithfully.*

Many people nowdays often add an extra line before the "Yours sincerely", and this is usually something like *With kindest regards,* or *With very best wishes.* I would only add the latter if I knew quite well the person to whom I was writing.

Contact Names

Letters to businesses are now generally much more informal than they used to be. However, there is a danger that if you become too familiar too soon, it could be difficult if you then have to write a more formal letter (of complaint, perhaps) which really ought to begin "Dear Sir".

That said, I still prefer to address my letters to a specific contact 'name'. The most important reason for doing so is that you are, in my opinion, more likely to receive a reply. If you don't, or something goes wrong, you always have someone with whom you can get in touch.

A contact name, or even a department name, is particularly useful when corresponding with big organisations where, if you write a general "Dear Sir" letter, it can get passed from department to department never to be seen again!

I would add here, that there is often an interminable delay when waiting for a reply from large organisations and you frequently have to be very patient! However, it is essential that you are persistent because some businesses (apart from their obvious inefficiency) may use 'delaying tactics' in the hope that you will become tired and abandon your correspondence. Keep on writing and referring to previous letters, and the fact that you have still not had a satisfactory reply, etc. And do not give up — however long it takes!

For The Attention Of ...
Technically, there are two different ways to start a letter when writing to someone in particular at a company. The first is:

> 10 Beeches Road
> LONDON
> SW13 5UB

Mr Peter Hardwick   *(the date)*
Green Fingers Garden Supplies
12 The Clears
TONBRIDGE
Kent
TN20 6XY

Dear Mr Hardwick

(You would close with "Yours sincerely".)

If you are writing a letter *For The Attention Of* a specific person at a company, you should set your letter out as follows:

10 Beeches Road
LONDON
SW13 5UB

Mr Peter Hardwick   *(the date)*
Green Fingers Garden Supplies
12 The Clears
TONBRIDGE
Kent
TN20 6XY

Dear Sirs

<u>For the attention of: Mr Peter Hardwick</u>

(You would sign yourself "Yours faithfully".)

When addressing an envelope for either of these two letters, the Post Office require any "For the attention of ..." information to be placed either *above* the address or to the left of it. It should not be put beneath the last line of the address. Thus you would put "Mr Peter Hardwick" or "For the attention of Mr Peter Hardwick" above the address.

Numbering Your Pages
If you are writing a letter of more than one page, you should always start each page on a fresh piece of paper; never use the back of the page. (This rule need not apply when writing social letters. See page 85.) There is no need to number the first page as it will be obvious from the address information at the top that this is where the letter begins. The top of each subsequent sheet should be set out like this:

Mr James Williams   – 2 –   *(the date)*
Williams & Co Ltd

The reason for putting the name (and company, if appropriate) of the recipient, with the date, is that if your pages become separated both you and the recipient will know to whom and when the information refers.

In addition to this heading on your continuation pages, you

could also put a small prompt at the bottom of each page where there is a page to come after it. For example, at the bottom of page 1 you could put:

2/...

this would indicate to the reader that there is another page to follow.

When you have finished, it is always wise to staple the pages together, as this way they are less likely to become separated.

Signing Off

All letters should be hand-signed. You should also type your name, or write it clearly in capitals, in addition to your signature. This is even more important if your signature is difficult to read, or, as in many cases, illegible!

Keeping Copies Of Correspondence

It is very important to keep copies of official letters (a complaint letter, or a letter to the bank, for example), as these may be needed in the future as proof of action or decision. They also serve you as excellent memory aids.

One method of keeping copies is by using carbon paper, and the type you can buy today is not nearly as messy as it used to be! Use flimsy paper for your copies; it is cheaper than the better quality paper you would use for actual letters.

A very useful product for doing copies is self-carboning copy paper which, as its name suggests, needs no carbon paper. It is generally available from good stationery shops.

Another way to keep copies is to photocopy your finished letters. If you do not have direct access to a copier, many libraries, high street stationers and print shops have a photocopying service available for a small charge.

Conclusion

The information above is designed to give you the basic guidelines for setting out and beginning your official letters.

The main points to remember are that these letters should contain all the relevant facts and information. They must be able to reach the correct person and be acted upon, and you must have good copies for your own future reference.

8

SIMPLE OFFICIAL LETTERS

In this chapter I have included a selection of simple letters covering a wide range of fairly common situations. I have shown a typewritten layout with *open punctuation* − see page 18.

Quote For Flooring
This is a very simple letter to a company, requesting a quote for floor covering.

Dear Mr Henderson

Further to our visit to your showroom on Saturday, my wife and I have now decided on the hardwood parquet flooring and would like you to give us a quote to have the work done.

Our room measures approximately 5 metres by 4 metres but it would obviously be better if you could call round to measure up and to see exactly what the size is.

We will be at home any afternoon next week, so would look forward to seeing you then. Perhaps you could give us a call on the day to let us know what time you expect to arrive.

Yours sincerely

Bank Standing Order
A very common letter is one to your bank requesting the setting up of a standing order facility. This letter would normally be sent to "The Manager" who would then pass it on to the appropriate department.

Dear Sir

I would be grateful if you could arrange for a standing order of £20 to be transferred from my current account, number 23657987, to my building society savings account. The money should be transferred to:

Account Name	:	Stephen J Arrowsmith
Account No.	:	31416898
Building Society	:	The Hanover Building Society 10 Bridge Street MANCHESTER M3 8DX

Could transfers please be made on the first working day of every month, beginning in *(month)* and continuing until further notice.

I look forward to your confirmation of this.

Yours faithfully

It is obviously important that when giving such instructions, you put the date on your letter; you should really date *ALL* your letters as advised in the previous chapter.

School – Letter Explaining Absence
At some time, most parents will be required to write to their child's school teacher advising them of illness. The following is an example of such a letter:

Dear Miss Blackwell

I am writing to let you know that Tim will be unable to attend school this week as he has chicken-pox.

We had to call the doctor out to him on Friday evening as he was poorly and had started to develop spots. The doctor has said that we must keep him in isolation for seven days; so I would therefore expect him to be back at school next Monday or Tuesday.

With best wishes.

Yours sincerely

Thanks For A Service Rendered

Although a high standard of service should be given by any company, it is unfortunate that this is not always the case. It is therefore a nice thought to write to someone when you have received particularly good service. Such a letter follows.

Dear Mr Dickens

I just wanted to send a note to say how very much my wife and I appreciate all the trouble you have gone to on our behalf to get the Texturelux wallpaper.

As you know, we had been all over the place trying to get this paper and it was not until we came into your shop that we received any sort of service. All too often nowadays, people are ready to criticise and complain, but can never be bothered to send a letter of praise and thanks when they receive the kind of excellent service such as my wife and I have from you. I am therefore sending a copy of this letter to your managing director so that he is aware of what a dedicated and willing salesman he has working in his company.

Once again, our grateful thanks.

Yours sincerely

Sending For Goods By Mail Order

Nowadays, many of us buy goods by mail order which we may

have seen advertised in magazines or catalogues. An example of a letter requesting such goods is given below.

Dear Sirs

I was interested to read your advertisement in this week's *Woman's Realm*, and would be most grateful if you could send me a king-size duvet set in "Peaches and Cream", as mentioned. Enclosed is a cheque for the required amount.

Could you also please let me have your latest brochure and price list (including any postage charges) showing your complete range of curtains and soft furnishings in this design, as I think it is lovely and would like to co-ordinate my room around it.

I look forward to hearing from you.

Yours faithfully

Advising Businesses When You Move House

If you are moving house there are many businesses and institutions who will need to know your new address, for example, the bank, building society, any clubs or societies to which you may belong, etc. To save you time, you could just type out one letter and have it photocopied. Such a letter could be based on the following:

Dear Sirs

Ref: *(any account number; membership number, etc.)*

I am writing to advise you that I am moving home. From the 12th of *month*, my new address will be:

> 4 Glovers Road
> PETERBOROUGH
> Cambs
> PE4 8BU

Could you please amend your records accordingly.

Yours faithfully

Once you have photocopied your 'master' copy, you can then fill in the relevant information, where necessary, on the photocopies.

Requesting Overdraft From Bank
This letter would be addressed to the manager, either by name if you know it, or by title.

Dear Sir *(or Dear Mr Briggs)*

You may be aware that in the last couple of months my account has become a little overdrawn, and I am writing to ask if I may have an overdraft facility of £200.

My reason for this request is that I have just had to pay out for my car insurance and it was a little more than I anticipated.

As you know, my salary is paid directly into my account on the 30th of each month, so funds will be paid in on a regular basis, and I would expect this overdraft to be cleared by the end of next month.

I do hope you will be able to send me a favourable reply and I look forward to hearing from you in due course.

Yours faithfully *(or Yours sincerely)*

Requesting Information From A College
Another example of a simple official letter is one to a college requesting information on a course which they run.

Dear Sir or Madam

For some time now I have been interested in doing a day-release course in joinery and carpentry.

I understand that you run such a course and I would be grateful to receive your latest prospectus and list of fees, together with any other relevant information. Enclosed is an s.a.e. for your convenience.

Yours faithfully

(An s.a.e. is a stamped addressed envelope to yourself.)

Confirming A Hotel Booking

You may have to write to a hotel or guest house confirming a booking for holiday accommodation. If you are writing to a large hotel, it is worth marking the letter (and envelope) "For The Attention Of: Reservations". When writing to a small guest house, it is probably sufficient to send your letter to the proprietor, as I have done in the following example:

Dear Mrs Burridge

Further to our telephone conversation today, I am pleased to confirm my booking for a double room with private bathroom for seven nights from 6th-11th September inclusive.

My wife and I will require bed, breakfast and evening meal facilities during our stay, and, as discussed, you will let us have a room with a sea view, if possible.

Enclosed is a cheque for the 10% deposit, and we look forward to seeing you all at Clifftops again in September.

With kindest regards and best wishes.

Yours sincerely

Courtesy Letter Thanking For Quotation

If you receive several quotations for the same job, it is always courteous to drop a line to those who were not successful in securing the job but who have, nevertheless, spent time on preparing their quotation. Such a letter could be as follows:

Dear Sirs

Thank you so much for sending the written quotation for the work which needs doing on my roof.

I have had several quotes for the repairs and I am afraid to say that I will not, on this occasion, be able to use your company to carry out the work. However, I just wanted to let you know the position and to thank you for your time and trouble.

Yours faithfully

You will notice that most of the letters in this section are quite short and to the point. It is always helpful to the reader (and it can save confusion) if your letters are concise.

9

OFFICIAL LETTERS REQUIRING MORE THOUGHT

As its name suggests, this chapter is concerned with letters which need more care, as very often the subject under discussion is of a sensitive nature. Or it could be that you are dissatisfied with a service of some kind and need to put your grievances in writing.

It may be worth mentioning that with this type of situation it is often better to try and deal with the matter verbally. The reasons are that it is generally a much more amicable way of handling a potential problem. If someone suddenly gets a letter (of complaint for example), the tone of the letter could actually make matters worse! There is also the time factor to take into account. If you deal with a matter verbally, you will know immediately where you stand, whereas if you send a letter there is always a period of delay while you wait for a reply.

However, there are times when something has to be put in writing, or a serious matter dealt with by correspondence. Very often, letters of this kind need to be longer than usual so that all the facts are laid out before the recipients to enable them to have a clear idea of the problem. It is therefore a good idea to keep notes of any meetings or telephone conversations so that all the relevant information is at your fingertips should you need to itemise certain points in a letter.

When writing such letters, it is worth bearing in mind:

(a) Do not write until you have calmly considered.
(b) Be courteous and concise, but you may need to be firm.
(c) Be patient and, if necessary, persistent.
(d) Don't worry *after* you have sent your letter.

I would *always* keep copies of this type of letter in order to refer back should the need arise. Keeping copies is especially important if you are threatening to take the matter further — to your solicitor, for example. (Also see **Keeping Copies of Correspondence** on page 47.)

The following are examples of letters covering a number of 'difficult' situations.

Complaint — Faulty Goods

Dear Sir

I was rather hoping that I would not have to write this letter, but I have been messed around so much by your staff that I feel the situation warrants a formal letter of complaint.

Last month I bought an electric kettle from your shop. Ever since getting it home it has been leaking, and despite my coming back about it several times your salesmen seem extremely reluctant to replace it.

Your Mr Greensmith initially offered to have it repaired for me, and although not happy with this arrangement, I agreed. The kettle was gone for over three weeks and when it was returned it worked satisfactorily for five days, before it began leaking again. When I returned it, Mr Greensmith offered to send it away again for repair. I told him that the situation had gone far enough and that I wanted a new appliance.

You were out when I called and, to my astonishment, I was told by Mr Greensmith that he would have to consult you before a decision could be made, as your company policy is not to replace appliances which were bought more than a month ago. I pointed out to him that I had, in fact, brought the kettle back as faulty after only two days!

This is how the situation now stands, and I personally feel that this is a wholly unsatisfactory way of doing business; to say nothing of the damage to customer goodwill.

I will be calling into your shop on Friday and I will expect a new replacement kettle to be waiting for me. I trust you will advise your staff of these arrangements.

Yours faithfully

Complaint — To M.P. And To Local Council
On occasion, you may have to write to your M.P. or local council and I give below examples of letters to both of these. If you have to write to your M.P., have a look at Chapter 4 for the correct way to address him or her.

Dear Sir

I have just come out of the Harlington Hospital and such is my concern with the conditions there that I felt I must inform you, as it could have far-reaching effects on other people in your constituency.

I was only in the hospital for three days while I had a minor operation on my foot, however, my three days were spent in what I can only describe as a dreadfully overcrowded, dirty ward (Craighouse Ward).

This may seem an exaggeration, but I can assure you that it is not. The ward was not only untidy and badly-kept — for example, dinner plates left uncleared for two hours on more than one occasion — but the sanitary facilities were disgusting. If I was presented with such facilities in a hotel, I would report it to the Health Inspector. Not only was there a general lack of cleanliness, but the food was horrendous. It was always lukewarm, badly cooked and totally unappetising — a bacterial paradise!

The doctors and nurses were very good indeed but were so obviously understaffed, and consequently overworked, that they were clearly unable to cope with the demands being put upon them.

I do hope you will investigate this matter urgently, as I feel the basic general hygiene of the hospital *must* be below the standard required. If this matter is not put right soon, I fear it could have serious consequences for elderly or very sick patients who could easily contract a serious infection as a result.

Yours faithfully

The following is a letter to the local council complaining about unkempt footpaths:

Dear Sirs

I have lived in Lower Meadington for over 20 years and was always proud of the way our town looked — until now. Over the last couple of years I have noticed a steady decline in standards on our highways and by-ways.

The footpaths in the town are now badly in need of repair. They are totally overgrown with weeds — not to mention all the accumulated rubbish. They are a major hazard to children and to the elderly who could easily have a serious accident. We now have an additional problem with wet leaves decaying in huge heaps along the paths, too. These could also cause an accident especially now that we have had so much rain in the last few days.

Could you please offer an explanation as to why our footpaths have been allowed to fall into such a state of disrepair and neglect? And, more importantly, what your department intends to do to rectify the situation.

I look forward to receiving your reply by return.

Yours faithfully

A copy of this letter should also be sent to your local councillor. Mention of this should be made in the form "Copy to..." below your signature.

Letter Supporting An Insurance Claim

A fairly common letter is one to an insurance company supporting a claim. In this example, the writer is querying why his insurers have declined to pay the full amount for a coat which has been completely destroyed by fire.

Dear Sirs

In reply to your letter offering £75 compensation against the coat which was recently burned, and which had been bought two months ago for £225, I must ask you to reconsider the matter.

In twenty-one years I have never made a claim and have paid you in premiums many hundreds of pounds. Do you consider your offer of £75 against a coat worth £225 is fair?

I did not claim the larger sum with any intention of entering into negotiation for its reduction, because the coat had only been worn twice and was obviously still worth its original value, or within a few pounds of it.

Unless you send the £225 within the next ten days, my policy will be transferred to another insurer, and I will be instructing my solicitor to take legal action to recover the £225 from your company.

I await your reply and trust that it will contain an explanation that some mistake has been made by your office.

Yours faithfully

It is worth mentioning that unless you really intend going to your solicitor, do not make the threat. In other words, never indicate that you will do something unless you are prepared to do it. The same would apply to the next example.

Complaint – Neighbour's Noisy Dog

You may be in the unenviable position of having to write a letter of complaint to a neighbour. This one deals with the problem of a neighbour's noisy dog. I have started the letter "Dear Mr. ...", but you could start it "Dear Gerald", or whatever, if the person is someone you know very well.

Dear Mr Molton

On several occasions I have mentioned to you that your dog's constant barking during the night is causing us a great deal of disturbance.

I was hoping that we could settle this matter amicably, but it now seems to me that you are totally unable or unwilling to control your animal.

I am writing, therefore, to inform you that if a solution to this problem is not forthcoming within the next seven days, I very much regret that I will have no choice but to put the matter in the hands of my solicitor.

Yours sincerely

Child Being Bullied At School

Another difficult situation in which you may need to write a letter could be where your child is being bullied at school. The example I have given is where the bullying is being done by a teacher, so a letter is being written "In Strictest Confidence" (envelope the same) to the head. You could adapt this letter if your child was being bullied by another pupil.

Dear Mr Jenkinson

Over the last few weeks I have become increasingly concerned about Jeremy. His school work has deteriorated and he has been sullen and withdrawn at home. Despite my trying to talk to him about this on numerous occasions, he would not discuss it with me.

However, things came to a head last night, and to my horror I discovered the reason for Jeremy's change in character is that one of your teachers is bullying and belittling him — both publicly and in private. The teacher in question is John Leonard — Jeremy's new maths teacher. When I asked Jeremy why he was being victimised in this way, he felt it was because he was not very good at maths and was falling behind most of his classmates in the subject. (However, it would appear that there are two others who are also being penalised in this way.)

As I am sure you will appreciate, these are very serious allegations, however I have no reason to disbelieve my son. I know that you will want to investigate this matter thoroughly and may need to interview both Jeremy and myself, and we will be pleased to discuss the matter further with you at any time.

However, I would like to receive your assurance, by return, that this matter will be looked into immediately. Also, I must insist that Jeremy is removed at once from this teacher's classes.

I would like to add that I will not tolerate a situation such as this, and if my son continues to be victimised in this way I will not only remove him from your school, but I will feel duty-bound to inform the school governors and the local education authority of my reasons for doing so.

I look forward to receiving your reply.

Yours sincerely

Defaulting On Mortgage Repayments
Finally I deal with a letter which we all hope we will never have to write; about defaulting on mortgage repayments. It is worth bearing in mind that if you find yourself in such a situation, a letter like this is better written sooner rather than later, as it is most unwise to let matters like this drift on and on. However, in my example letter, I am assuming that the writer has been hoping things would get better, which is why he has put off writing his letter.

Dear Mr Crawford

I sincerely regret having to write this letter, and have been delaying it in the hope that things would improve. However, as the outlook is still very bleak, I felt it best to get in touch and put you in the picture.

The problem, quite simply, is that my wife and I are finding it impossible, at present, to keep up with the current level of mortgage repayments on our home.

Two months ago, I was made redundant (I was given one week's notice) from my job which I had held for over fifteen years. As you can appreciate, it has not been easy trying to find alternative employment in the same trade, and now, in desperation, I have taken a job working at the local hypermarket. The problem is that my wages are now a third less than they used to be, and because we are already behind with our repayments I can see no way that we can 'catch up' again, let alone pay the money we are now in arrears. My wife can only work part-time, and the money she earns is spent on feeding the family.

I am very sorry about this, and wondered if it would be possible for us to meet and discuss the situation. Perhaps we could work something out whereby my wife and I could pay you a reduced amount, but over a longer period, or something of that sort.

Once again, my sincere apologies for all of this, but I hope we can meet and get it sorted out very soon.

Yours sincerely

10

APPLYING FOR A JOB

A letter applying for a job is probably one of the most important you will ever have to write; and its style, presentation and content could have a strong bearing on the decisions of any potential employer.

When applying for a job, the state of your handwriting is often considered to be a reflection of your personality. A neatly-written, well set out letter could make the difference between your getting an interview or not. In some jobs, neat handwriting is of vital importance, for instance in occupations where legible and tidily-written numbers are imperative.

If you have several qualifications and a good deal of work experience, you may wish to compose your own Curriculum Vitae (C.V.). This is a brief resumé of the schools/colleges you have attended with qualifications gained, together with personal information and brief details of your career to date.* It would be quite correct to send a typed C.V., but it is worth noting that most employers would prefer to see it accompanied by a handwritten covering letter.

There are, however, still a few occasions when a letter, containing all the relevant information, could be used in preference to a C.V.

When writing a letter of this kind, the secret is to be brief and to the point. Try only to include information which is relevant to the job for which you are applying. Don't write page after page of waffle, with details which will be of no interest to the reader, or your letter is likely just to be cast aside. An over long letter giving vast details of your past and present life

---

*Further details on compiling a C.V. are given in the Right Way companion *THE RIGHT WAY TO WRITE YOUR OWN C.V.*

will probably count against you.

One of the most common ways in which we hear about job vacancies is through newspaper advertisements, and these would normally require a letter of application. Before replying, read the advertisement with great care and make sure that all the information requested is supplied in your answer.

Here are some sample advertisements followed by appropriate replies, to give you an idea of what is required.

(a) Advertisement

Senior P.A. required for young art director of international ad. agency. Needs someone to organise him totally and look after the office when he's away. First class shorthand and typing speeds, W.P. and organisational skills essential. Ad. agency experience preferred. Age 25+. Excellent salary for right person. Contact Jason Davies, Personnel Manager, Actionads Ltd., 3 Wray's Walk, Croydon, Surrey CR9 0LS.

Reply

Dear Mr Davies

Further to your advertisement in yesterday's Croydon Courier for a senior P.A., I would very much like to be considered for this vacancy.

I am 28 years old, and have worked as a senior level P.A. for the past eight years; most recently for John Charlton, art director of Artlines Advertising Agency in London. Although I have been very happy at Artlines for the past four years, I now feel that I would like to have a job which is nearer to my new home in Purley.

For the last eleven years I have worked exclusively in advertising, so feel that the experience I have gained will be of great value in your company.

In my present job I regularly cover for Mr Charlton in his absence, when I am responsible for the day-to-day running of the office, the answering of correspondence, and the supervision of two junior members of our support team.

After leaving Croydon High School with eight G.C.S.E.s, I studied for two years at The Lawns Secretarial College in Selhurst, where I gained certificates for 100 w.p.m. shorthand, and advanced level typing. My present shorthand and typing speeds are 110 w.p.m. and 70 w.p.m. respectively, and I have a good working knowledge of Microsoft Windows 95, Word 6, Word Perfect 8 and Excel software.

I do hope to hear from you soon.

Yours sincerely

(b) Advertisement

Lady or gentleman required for school crossing patrol at St. Mark's Junior School, Swindon. Would suit active senior citizen. Hours: 8.00–9.15 a.m. and 3.00–4.15 p.m., Monday–Friday. Uniform provided. Excellent rates of pay. Please contact The Works Manager, Swindon District Council, The Town Hall, 23 High Street, Swindon, Wilts., SN8 9AG.

Reply

Dear Sir

I am writing with regard to your vacancy for a school crossing patrol person at St. Mark's Junior School, as advertised in this week's Swindon Messenger.

Since retiring last December I have been looking for a suitable part-time job and feel that your vacancy is ideal, as St. Mark's is just round the corner from where I live. I do not have any other regular commitments on my time, so I could easily be available during the hours which you state.

I know many of the parents whose children attend St. Mark's, as my two grandchildren are pupils there.

Before I retired, I was a traffic warden for fifteen years, so I am well aware of road safety and traffic regulations which I think would be useful in this post.

My hobbies are walking, gardening and D.I.Y. and I consider myself to be very fit and active for my age.

I do hope that I will be successful, and that I may hear from you in the near future.

Yours faithfully

(c) Advertisement

Gardener required for about two days a week for a one-acre garden in Colchester. Small orchard, vegetable plot, greenhouse and flower beds to tend. All equipment provided. Hours to suit. Excellent rates of pay, plus meals and share of produce. Please reply to Box 35, Colchester Courier Newspaper Group, 254 Green Street, Colchester, Essex. CO1 1YY.

Reply

Dear Sir or Madam

I was most interested to read your advertisement for a gardener, and feel I could be just the person for your vacancy.

Ten months ago, I moved to Colchester from Norwich where I had been employed for four years as a landscape gardener with Logan Landscapes. I also have a Certificate in Horticultural Studies.

Since moving to Colchester, I have been a self-employed jobbing gardener, but I now have two days a week to spare since one of the people I worked for has died.

Should you require a reference, please feel free to get in touch with Mr David Logan at Logan Landscapes, 10 Quarry Street, Norwich, Norfolk, NR5 9BU, who will be happy to help you.

I look forward to hearing from you soon.

Yours faithfully

(d) Advertisement

Junior required to work in friendly office/warehouse. Work will include filing, photocopying, packing orders and general office duties. Age 16-19. Good general education required, but no qualifications or experience necessary as full training will be given. Good starting salary with reviews every six months.

Please apply to Mr Peter Endell, The Redbridge Clothing Company, Redbridge Road, Liverpool, L45 8UX.

Reply

Dear Mr Endell

With reference to your advertisement in today's Liverpool Times, I would very much like to be considered for the vacancy of office junior in your company.

I am 16 years old and will be leaving Middleham School at the end of next week, as I will then have finished my five G.C.S.E. examinations.

For the past year I have worked as a Saturday sales assistant at Charisma Fashions in Liverpool who stock many of your lines, so I am quite familiar with your range of garments. Mrs Grant, the manageress at Charisma, has offered to give me a reference if you require one.

It has always been my wish to have a career in the clothing industry, and I would be grateful for the opportunity to talk to you about the vacancy you have available.

I do hope that I may be considered for the job, and that you may invite me for interview in the near future.

Yours sincerely

Applying For An Unadvertised Job

There is no doubt, of course, that many positions are filled which are never advertised. Sometimes one hears of jobs which are open or likely to be open, and a visit to the employer may prove successful. In other cases, a letter may have to be written, and it should be kept short and give brief but full particulars. The letter could be composed in a variety of ways, and here is an example.

Dear Sirs

I have heard from a friend that you are likely to be requiring an invoice clerk and I am taking the liberty of writing, as I would be very interested should a vacancy arise. Below are particulars of my previous experience:

The details can then be listed and that is all there is to it. Conclude with:

I do hope to hear from you and I enclose a stamped addressed envelope for your reply.

Yours faithfully

Applying For A Job In Another District

There is also the case where someone may need to move to a new district and have to find employment in a particular trade. The best way is probably to write to the companies in the trade you wish to enter (if there are not too many of them) in the new locality, and an example of such a letter is given below:

Dear Sirs

I will soon be moving into your area from Dorset and am writing to enquire whether you have any vacancies for retail hi-fi sales staff within your company. I have a wide experience in this business, and I am therefore hoping to continue my employment in this field. Full particulars of my previous experience are given below: (*list of particulars*)

You could conclude:

I would be most grateful to hear if there is any opening in your firm for which I might be suitable. Failing that, I would be obliged if you could advise me of any other firms to whom you think it might be worth while my writing. I enclose a stamped addressed envelope and thank you in anticipation.

Yours faithfully

11

INTRODUCTIONS,
REFERENCES
AND RESIGNATIONS

INTRODUCTIONS

Although these are rarely used nowadays, it is still useful to know
a bit about them.

When writing an introductory letter, always take great care
to ensure that the wording is accurate so that no false assumptions
can be arrived at by the recipient. Considerable importance might
be attached to the fact that you had gone to the trouble of giving
an introduction, and it might be thought that because of this you
knew the party to be absolutely reliable, which might not always
be the case.

Below is an example of a letter of introduction for someone
that the writer knows very well who has emigrated.

Dear Peter and Jenny,

I do hope you and the boys are all well and that life "Down-
Under" is keeping you all busy.

My reason for writing is that some of my close friends have just
moved out to Australia and, coincidentally, are living in
Melbourne. Their names are Roger and Jackie Brampton. I have
known them for over ten years and they were, in fact, my next
door neighbours for six years. They have three children — Emma
(8), Billy (5) and Sam (2). Roger is a civil engineer and has
got a job in Melbourne working for S.C.G., which I believe is
the biggest engineering firm there. The company have found
them a house, and their address is: Box 63, Wongalong Road,
Melbourne.

As they have no relatives or friends in Australia, I said I would write and ask if you would get in touch with them. Maybe you could give them a few hints about the locality and that sort of thing? It would really help them get started. I know you'll love them — they're a smashing family!

I would be so grateful if you'd do this for me, and look forward to hearing how you all get along.

Will write a long letter soon.

With love and best wishes ...

Another type of introductory letter might be one written for someone seeking employment, but apart from this, most other forms of introduction would probably be done over the telephone; for example, you might introduce a friend to a reputable firm of builders.

REFERENCES

It would be impossible to overstress the importance of the wording of a reference letter, because a great deal can depend upon it.

Basically, there are two types of reference. There is the reference (more correctly known as a testimonial) which someone leaving takes with them, and I feel that this is not really worth much unless the recipient knows something about the writer of the reference. My reason for this is simply that it is always assumed that a lot of praise is put into the letter, possibly more out of kindness than because it is deserved.

The other, more valuable, reference is the one which is obtained by the prospective employer writing direct to the former employer asking any particular questions he might wish answered. There is, however, a potential danger here that an employer could write a good reference for an employee because he wants to be rid of him (or her)! Generally speaking, though, employers are fair-minded and give an honest reference — to protect their professional integrity if nothing else!

Having said that, I personally never attach too much value to any reference, the reason being that although a person may have done badly in a previous job, it does not follow that he will do badly in the next one. Working conditions may vary and such is the nature of personal relationships that employees who cannot work satisfactorily for one person, very often can for another. Also, it often follows that if an employee has not done very well in a previous job, he has learnt a lesson and will do much better in the new one.

The Writing Of References

Business people today usually want a concise summary of the individual concerned. I would think that the old-fashioned type of reference, several pages long, which was concerned with things like length of service, qualities of character and so on, is rarely used nowadays. Many larger companies often just send out a standard questionnaire for the former employer to fill in.

If you are ever asked to write a reference you should be guided by the following points:

    (a) absolute accuracy

    (b) brevity.

Another very important point it is worth noting is that *all* reference letters should be marked "Private & Confidential", as should the envelopes in which you send them.

Below are some different examples of the sort of wording you could use if writing references for good employees.

(a) Catrina Kelly is leaving us as our secretary as she is moving away from this area. She is a conscientious and dedicated member of our team and her work has always been excellent.

(b) Darren Gale is leaving us because his career has advanced as far as possible within our company. He has been in charge of our buying department for three years and has been a very able and competent manager. We have no vacancy higher up so cannot give him the promotion he deserves. We are very sorry to lose him, but wish him every success in the future.

(c) Joanna Black has been our senior sales manager for five years and is leaving us because our wholesale department has been sold. We are very pleased to be able to say that Joanna has injected enormous energy and flair into all her projects, and we have no hesitation in recommending her for your vacancy.

This type of reference is comparatively easy, but we now come to the problem of giving a reference to a person who has been less satisfactory as an employee. This is a very difficult matter because naturally an employer does not like to condemn someone who may have been unsatisfactory in the past. The best line to take with somebody who has not been *too bad* is to write something like:

Simon Green is leaving us because he needs a higher salary than we feel able to pay him. He has been with us for two years and we have always found him trustworthy and wish him success in the future.

There is also the much more difficult instance of the employee who has been dishonest and thoroughly unsatisfactory. If such an employee asks you for a reference he can take away with him when he leaves, the best thing to do is to refuse to give one, but to say that you are willing to supply one to a prospective employer.

If you do this it is extremely unlikely that the person concerned will ever give your name to a future employer because he would not expect a good reference, and if he is dishonest he will probably make up some story or provide a bogus reference. (It might interest you to know that the employees who have swindled me, and there have been a few, were the ones who provided the most wonderful references as to their integrity, etc.)

In giving an adverse reference regarding an employee, you would be entitled to state the facts fully but accurately, provided the letter is addressed personally to the enquirer. It is most important in this instance that the letter (and envelope) be marked "Private & Confidential". However, you must be extremely cautious when writing references of this nature. Even in a confidential letter, if anything was said which was out of malice or spite, however tempted you might be, the legal position might prove very dangerous. (See **Dangers Of The Written Word** page 31.)

If you find yourself in a position where you have to give an adverse reference, let me offer you a word of advice. It is always much better to give a bad reference by word of mouth than in writing, and the line to take is to tell the truth about the person, but without malice, as even verbally, the legal position is always uncertain.

RESIGNATIONS

The most important thing to say about resignations is that they are often accepted, therefore do not resign from something in a fit of temper if you do not really want to.

Below is an example of a resignation letter which you may write to an employer when you wish to leave your job. This type of letter is quite straightforward to write and should be as concise as possible.

Dear Mr Harrison

It is with much regret that I have to write and inform you of my wish to resign from my current position. I have always enjoyed my work with your company, but feel that the time has come when I would like to have a job in a new field. I have been offered a vacancy locally, so would like to leave in one month's time, as required by my contract.

Yours sincerely

If you have to resign from the committee of a club or society, this is dealt with in the next chapter.

12

LOCAL CLUBS AND SOCIETIES AND LETTERS TO "THE EDITOR"

LOCAL CLUBS & SOCIETIES

Many of us are members of clubs and societies in our local areas — squash or tennis clubs, conservation groups, amateur dramatic societies, family history societies, over-60s clubs — the choice is many and varied.

Applying For Membership

The procedure for joining these various activities will vary from group to group, but I will start by giving a simple letter which you could use when applying for membership of, say, a local squash club. This letter would be sent to the Membership Secretary.

Dear Sir or Madam

I have just moved to this area and am writing to enquire whether I may become a member of the Brayside Squash Club.

My standard of play is generally thought to be better than average, as I am currently top of the second division in the Club league at the Calverley Squash Club in north London, where I have been a member for the last three years.

Please could you let me know if there is a waiting list, as I am most anxious to join your club right away. I would be grateful if you could let me know your annual fee charges and any other information which would be useful.

I look forward to hearing from you in the near future. Please find enclosed a stamped, self-addressed envelope for your reply.

Yours faithfully

You will note from the above that the writer sends an s.a.e. with his letter. I firmly believe that this can make a big difference. Not only will it speed up the postal side of your reply, but people often feel 'obliged' to reply to you! It could also mean that your letter may be put to the top of the pile for reply. There are, in fact, many reasons why sending an s.a.e. is a good idea, not least that it is a courteous gesture which is usually much appreciated by the recipient.

Joining A Committee
There may come a time when you are asked to join the committee of a local group, or you may volunteer and be elected at its Annual General Meeting. Depending on your rôle, you may have to correspond with various people on behalf of the group.

Booking A Guest Speaker
As a member of a committee, you may be responsible for booking guest speakers, who should always get a confirmatory letter. An example of such a letter follows.

Dear Mr Jarvis

Further to our telephone conversation, I am delighted that you have kindly agreed to give an illustrated talk to our Group on the subject of "Wildlife In Surrey", on the 6th of next month.

The meeting will be held at St. Peter's Hall, Lower Road, Redhill, starting at 8.00 p.m., so if you could arrive a few minutes before this it will give you time to get settled in.

We would be grateful if your talk could last approximately 30-45 minutes. After this, there will be a break for refreshments, followed by a questions session which usually lasts for about 30 minutes. You mentioned that you will not require a slide projector as you will be bringing all your own equipment.

As discussed, you do not require a fee for your talk, but would only need a small payment towards your travel expenses.

Finally, I enclose a sketch map showing how to get to the hall, and I very much look forward to seeing you next month. Please do not hesitate to get in touch if you need to discuss this further.

With very best wishes and thanks.

Yours sincerely

Mrs Jane T McFarlane
Programme Organiser
Surrey Hills Conservation Group

At the top of the letter you need to put your own address (unless the group has an 'official' address), and the address of the recipient; don't forget the date! It would also be helpful to them if you included your telephone number. If you have a phone number for the person to whom you are writing, it is always a good idea to jot this down on your copy of the letter. Also, note from the above how you should close a letter of this kind, putting your name, 'job' title and name of your group along with your signature. If your letter needs a reply, include an s.a.e.

You will see that my example contains *all* the information that may be needed in the future. The reason for this is that many such speakers (especially the best ones!) are booked up for months, and sometimes years, in advance. It is therefore vitally important that (a) such a confirmatory letter is sent, and (b) every scrap of information is included. With the passage of time, it is easy to forget the details of verbal arrangements. If you book a speaker a long way in advance, it is always wise to check nearer the time that they are still able to give the talk — either by sending a short follow-up letter, or by giving them a quick call.

Thanking A Guest Speaker
It is customary, and good manners, to write a short note of thanks to any guest speaker who may visit your group. This letter should always be sent the day after the talk. Remember to insert your name, position on the committee and name of the group at the bottom of the letter, as the speaker (especially if he/she is popular) may visit several groups each week. The following is an example of the type of letter which is required.

Dear Mrs Applegarth

On behalf of the ladies of the Lowfield W.I., I would just like to say how very much we enjoyed your talk yesterday evening. Not only was it highly amusing, but your floral creations were delightful.

Thank you so much for coming to speak to us, and I do hope you may be able to pay us a return visit in the future to talk to us about one of your other horticultural specialities.

With best wishes and thanks once again.

Yours sincerely

(you would then put your name, position, and the name of the group)

Leaving The Committee
There is bound to come a time when you will have to leave the committee. There may be various reasons — perhaps you cannot now spare the time, or you feel it's time to let someone else have a go, or maybe you are moving away from the area. I have used this last reason in the following example of a letter which could be used when you have to resign from a committee.

Dear Stuart

As you know, I am leaving the district in two months' time, so it is with great regret that I will have to resign as Secretary of the Downs Cricket Club.

I would like to take this opportunity to say how much I have enjoyed being a member of the committee; I shall miss all the very good friends I have made.

May I send you all my very best wishes for the future; I shall be keeping in touch so will continue to follow the Club's progress with interest!

Yours

This letter would be sent to the Chairman of the Committee.

There are obviously many other letters which you could write on behalf of a local group or society, but I hope the ones above demonstrate how to deal with the sort of detailed and unusual things you are likely to come across.

For the writing of more general letters, see Chapters 8 and 9.

LETTERS TO "THE EDITOR"

As the name suggests, these are letters covering a wide range of subjects which are written to the editors of national and regional newspapers, or magazines, by members of the public.

Generally speaking, it is very difficult to get a letter printed in a national daily newspaper and particularly in one of the "serious", "heavyweight" newspapers such as *The Times* or *The Daily Telegraph*. But people do, and if you are aspiring to this it is worth studying the formula which the letter writers use to put together a good, publishable letter. These serious papers often print quite long letters which deal with matters of a political or economic nature, with several aspects of a particular subject being under discussion.

Other national "dailies", such as *The Daily Mail* or *The Daily Express* carry letters which concern all manner of topical subjects. These letters tend to be shorter than those carried by the more serious papers, and generally deal with one point only, as this is usually all that space will allow.

By far the easiest place to get a letter to the editor published is in your local newspapers. Letters vary in length and are usually concerned with local issues about which many people feel very strongly.

When writing a letter to any newspaper it is worth remembering the following points.

(a) Always type your letter in double line spacing.

(b) Choose a subject that is topical and about which people will be interested to read.

(c) Be as concise as possible. Don't let your letter 'stray' to other irrelevant points, or its impact will be lost.

(d) Establish beyond doubt that your facts are absolutely correct and that you are not writing anything of a libellous nature (see Chapter 5).

(e) Before sending your letter, be completely sure in your own mind that you are prepared for it to be published. Remember, that in receiving your letter any editor would rightfully assume your automatic consent to its publication.

I have not included any examples of these letters in this book, as I believe that studying the letters in the various newspapers is by far the best way to learn what is required.

PART THREE

SOCIAL LETTERS

13
STARTING A SOCIAL LETTER

Presentation
Below are some useful tips to bear in mind when writing to friends and relatives:

1. Try to write as clearly and neatly as possible. We all like to receive letters and to enjoy the news they contain, but this pleasure is lessened if we have to spend a long time deciphering each word.
2. If you are writing to old people or to youngsters, don't write too small. Both groups will be able to read larger writing more quickly. Children also love the occasional drawing, even if you are a poor artist!
3. Quite a few people, especially those who do not write many letters, forget to insert the date, but I feel it is important to date *all* correspondence. Even on personal letters, it gives the reader a reference — especially if you use phrases like "last Saturday" or "next Wednesday".

Setting Out Your Social Letters
This section deals with the totally hand-written letter, i.e. one which is not written on printed notepaper. For more information on printed notepaper see Chapter 1, page 10.

Generally speaking, I would not type a letter to a friend, I would always try to hand-write it. I would also indent my paragraphs. See note on page 26. If you *have* to type a social letter (for instance if the letter is a very long one), I would apologise for the fact that it is typed, as some people could be slightly offended to receive a typed social letter.

When writing to friends, I would usually just put my own address, followed by the date, in the top right hand corner, and would not bother including my friend's address. I do not normally include my telephone number on letters of this kind unless I need an urgent response.

An example of this type of heading is as follows:

> The Green House,
> Tiverton Road,
> SWINDON,
> Wilts.
> SN3 4PP

> *(the date)*

One point worth noting in this heading is that the name of the house is not in inverted commas. Many people used to (and still do) put the name of the house in inverted commas. It is not really necessary to do this, although it would be a good idea if the name of the house also happened to be that of a town, as below:

> "Tavistock",
> Sandy Lane,
> READING,
> Berks.
> RG2 7AC

The alternative style of heading is the centred one, like the one above.

Opening And Closing

The opening is correctly called the *salutation* and is the "Dear ..." part of your letter, and the ending is called the *complimentary closing* and is the "Yours ..." part.

Most people have a telephone so, for instance, if you wanted to make arrangements to meet someone for lunch, or to fix up a game of squash, you are probably more likely to call than to write them a note.

However, a great many people still write letters to friends and relatives on their birthdays and at Christmas, or correspond with people living abroad, and it is useful to know how to start letters in these circumstances.

I always feel that when writing social letters, informality is the rule. But how you start your letter usually depends on how well you know the person to whom you are writing. Below are a few ideas for you to use as a guide when beginning your letters.

To A Parent/Parents: Usually, you would start with "Dear Mum/Dad", or "Dear Mum and Dad"; or, in speech, you may call them "Mummy" and "Daddy", in which case you may start "Dear Mummy and Daddy". I would think that rarely, nowadays, do people call their parents "Mother and Father", but if this were the case, again, you could begin "Dear Mother and Father".

If you are very close to your parents, you may wish to begin with the word "Dearest ...".

A friend of mine called her mum by a 'pet' name, which was "Poppet"! When writing to her, or sending her a greetings cards, she may have put "Dear Poppet". It would be quite O.K. to start your letter in this way if you call your parent/parents by an endearing 'pet' name.

To Grandparents or Brothers/Sisters: When writing to grandparents or to brothers/sisters, the same rules would apply as when writing to parents (see above).

To Aunts and/or Uncles: Just start, "Dear Auntie Pam", or "Dear Uncle John"; this should be correct. You may begin with "Dearest" instead of "Dear" if you are very close to your relative. This would also apply to unrelated older family friends whom you may call "Auntie" or "Uncle" in speech, but who are not, in fact, related.

To "The Other Half" (e.g. Wife/Husband, Engaged Couples, Boyfriend/Girlfriend): Again, "Dear Steve/Jackie" is usual, but some may wish to begin with, "My darling Steve/Jackie", or possibly just "Darling". I feel that romantic beginnings are probably more likely to be put into greetings cards than into letters.

Many couples have silly 'pet' names for each other and they may start with, "Dear ... *(followed by the 'pet' name)'*: You only have to look at the Valentine's Day greetings in newspapers to see the fantastic names couples dream up for each other!

Close Friends: Here again, "Dear James" would be correct. However, you may like to begin with "My Dear James". Or, if you prefer, you could start "Dearest Sue".

Adults To Their Children: "Dear Pippa" or "Dear Jamie" would be usual; although you may wish to start with "Dearest". The same would apply when writing to nieces or nephews. Again, it would be acceptable to start with a 'pet' name.

Youngsters To Youngsters: When youngsters are writing to each other "Dear Phil/Jan" would almost certainly be used.

Youngsters To Adults: When writing to an unrelated older person, you would generally use the same style as you would if writing to an aunt or uncle.

Youngsters would probably put "Dear Mr./Mrs. Brown", unless the person they were addressing was, say, an old unrelated family friend whom they called "Auntie/Uncle".

If the youngster was on first-name-terms with the adult to whom he/she was writing, they could put "Dear Mike/Jane".

The general rule is that anyone with whom you are not on first name terms should be addressed as "Dear Mr./Mrs.", that is unless they have a title or are a doctor or clergyman. For **Forms of Address And Subscription** see page 27.

Closing A Letter To All The Above Groups:
There are several ways in which you could close letters to the above, any of which would be suitable depending on your

relationship to the person being addressed.

Suitable endings are: "Love"; "With much love"; "With all my love"; "With my love and very best wishes"; "With very best wishes". All these should be followed by your first name.

When adults are writing to adult acquaintances, they might just sign off with "Yours", followed by their name.

If an elderly aunt were writing to a youngster she may sign off "Yours affectionately".

Signing Off

Generally, I would not print or type my name at the bottom of a letter to a friend or relative, as I would expect the recipient to know who had sent it. However, when signing off a letter to people you do not know very well, it is always a good idea to print your name in capitals underneath your signature so that they will know to whom they should reply.

Numbering Your Pages

When writing a letter of more than two pages, it is always sensible to number the pages so that your recipient has no difficulty in reading it. You do not have to start each page on a fresh sheet; it is acceptable to write on both sides of the paper.

There is no real need to number your first page, as it will be obvious, from the top of it that this is where your letter begins. Page 2 can be written on the back of the first page, then page 3 on a new page, with page 4 on the back of it, and so on.

Keeping Copies Of Correspondence

I would not generally keep copies of letters to friends, however, if you only write to someone once a year (at Christmas, for example) it might be a good idea to keep a copy of the letter so you can remember what you said last time!

The Technique Of The Longer Letter

Many people find the writing of a long letter a very difficult matter. However, the most important thing which the beginner has to learn is that a letter, to be really effective, should be written more or less as one would speak. In other words, do not sit down, look at the paper and think: "Oh dear, what can I *write?*", but just begin writing the letter as if you were talking to the person. In this way your letter will really come alive.

Another point to be remembered is that if you put yourself in the place of the recipient and try to think of the things he would like to find in the letter, you will get ideas as to what to write.

In long letters, try to avoid putting in extra words just for the sake of length, otherwise the letter is apt to be boring. Also remember that it greatly adds to the interest if you can quote what friends have said, or tell of a humorous happening to yourself or someone else. Human interest is generally more exciting than anything else.

Another factor creating a good letter is the avoidance of too much about the obvious. Fill your letter with as much unusual information as possible, particularly with material which you know will be of especial interest to the person receiving the letter.

14

THANKS AND THINGS

The "Thank You" letter is probably one of the easiest to write, because it is always easy to express gratitude.

The only problems that you might encounter are that your letter may not sound very sincere, or that it may appear too 'gushing'; what you should try to achieve is something between the two! The other problem is that you may find your letter is not long enough. It doesn't have to be a great long screed, but it shouldn't be too short or it could appear merely businesslike. If I am faced with this problem, I get round it by writing the "thank you" part in the first couple of paragraphs, then I extend the letter with another couple of paragraphs of news (i.e. what I've been doing, etc.).

Christmas Or Birthday Gift
One of the most common needs for a thank you letter is for a birthday or Christmas gift:

Dear Mum and Dad,

You shouldn't have! But how lovely that you did! I know we've already said thanks on the phone, but I just wanted to write, and again say thank you so very much for your wonderful present.

Imagine, a week in Paris! You'll never know how delighted Jane and I were when we opened the envelope on Christmas morning and found the two tickets inside. It was such a fantastic surprise!

How kind of you to think of it; you know how much we've been wanting a break, but with all our outgoings at the moment, a holiday just was totally out of the question.

Anyway, now that we've got our breath back, you must come over soon for the weekend. I'll call you next week so that we can fix up a date.

With all our love and thanks,

Wedding Presents
Another common occasion when a thank you letter is appropriate is for wedding presents. You can buy special cards for this occasion which are blank inside for your special message. As you will probably have quite a few people to write and thank, it is best to keep each note on the short side; if you write a long letter to each one, you'll be at it for days! The following gives you an idea of the type of information you could include:

Dear Auntie Pat and Uncle Stephen,

Thank you both so much for the beautiful duvet and linen set you gave Bob and me as a wedding present. They are already being put to good use, and look absolutely lovely in the bedroom now that we've finished decorating.

Our honeymoon in Rome was wonderful. Although I'm not sure we did everything the Romans do! The sun shone, and we both came back with a smashing tan. It really was the holiday of a lifetime. What a way to start married life!

However, we're back down to earth with a bump now and are surrounded by pots of paint, as we continue to do up the house. It's a labour of love, though, and everything is really starting to take shape.

Hope you are both keeping well and that we will see you again very soon.

With our love and best wishes,

Occasional Presents

Sometimes, you may be given a surprise gift "out of the blue" and although you would probably phone to say "thanks", there may be occasions when you feel that you would like to send a note. Here is an example:

Dear Paul and Sarah,

Sorry we missed you when you called, and how kind of you to bring us so many lovely plums from your tree. When we arrived home and saw the box on the doorstep, we wondered what on earth could be in it. When we saw all that fruit we were worried that you may not have kept enough for yourselves.

Oh, but they're *so* delicious. We've eaten lots of them already and Sally's in the kitchen at the moment making pies for the freezer, as well as freezing most of the remaining fruit so that I don't eat it all now!

It was a lovely thought and much appreciated, and I hope we'll be able to return the favour when our rhubarb crop comes up next year.

With our very best wishes and thanks,

Service Rendered

If someone does you a good turn it is more than likely that you will want to write them a letter of thanks. The following example is from a grateful patient who has just come out of hospital.

Dear Dr. Scott,

Now that I'm home and settled back in, I just had to write and thank you for making my stay in hospital such a comfortable one.

The dedication of you and your team, and the kindness of the sisters and nurses on Beauchamp Ward were unequalled. Your professionalism and efficiency was always evident and served as a great boost of confidence to all the patients.

With my grateful thanks and very best wishes to you all,

Thanks After Being Entertained

If you are invited for a meal or to stay for the weekend with friends, they will more than likely go to a lot of trouble on your behalf. It is therefore good manners (and will be appreciated) if you write a note of thanks. You could write something like:

Dear Mike and Caroline,

Just a quick note to say how very much we enjoyed our weekend with you; thanks so much for inviting us. The break did us the power of good, and what with the delicious home cooking and excellent company — well — we could have stayed forever!

Our journey home was very pleasant. We stopped off in the New Forest for a cream tea on our way back, and arrived here at about six o'clock.

Once again, many thanks for your hospitality and hope to see you both very soon.

With our love and best wishes.

LETTERS TO CHILDREN

As I advised earlier, always try to write as simply and clearly as possible. Children always want facts to the bitter end, and are not interested in possibilities and probabilities. Never leave an incident unfinished, and try also to keep the style of your letter very simple and easy to understand. For small children write as neatly as possible, and leave a gap between each letter, as it will be much easier for them to read.

The following are two letters which you could use as a guide if you have to write to children. The first is a thank you letter for a Christmas present:

Dear Peter,

Thank you so much for the lovely plant you got me for Christmas. I have put it on my table by the window and it looks really pretty.

Did you get lots of presents at Christmas? I know you were hoping to get some "Space Giants", and I hope you did.

We had a lovely surprise on Christmas morning when our cat, Blackie, had six kittens. They are still very small, but will soon be running about. Your mum has said that she will bring you over to see them on Saturday, so we will look forward to seeing you then.

With lots of love,

   The next example of a letter to a child is one wishing a little girl "Get Well".

Dear Jane,

I saw your dad in the supermarket tonight and he said that you were in bed poorly with mumps.

How horrible for you! I remember when I had it. But not to worry, you will soon be up and about, and you will have a nice few days off school while you get better.

John said he would like to cycle over to see you on Saturday, after Scouts. He had mumps last year so he will not be able to catch it again, and he would very much like to come round and cheer you up a bit.

We all hope you will soon be feeling much better.

Lots of love,

SENDING A GIFT

If you send a gift to someone, it is always a good idea to send a little note with it. (Otherwise, your friend may not realise who sent the present!) Such a letter could say:

Dear Christine,

I went up to London yesterday and was browsing round one of the big record stores there when I came across the enclosed cassette and just *had* to get it for you.

Isn't it a coincidence that only the other day we were talking about it and the problems you've had trying to get hold of a copy? I do hope you enjoy it.

Let me know if you want any other of his albums (they had a very wide selection), as I'll be going up there again next Monday.

With love and best wishes,

GREETINGS

If you are sending, for example, a Christmas card to friends overseas, you may feel that this alone is insufficient and that you would like to include a little note. The following is an example of the sort of thing you could write.

Dear Barry and Lyn,

Just a quick note to let you know we all remember and think about you both.

Hope you are still enjoying yourselves out there and we are all looking forward to seeing you when you come over for a holiday in the Summer. Things here are quite hectic in the run up to Christmas, so I will keep this note short and write you a long letter in the New Year to let you know what we've been up to.

Hope you all have a smashing Christmas, and we wish you every happiness in *date*.

With our love and best wishes,

15

GOOD LUCK AND CONGRATULATIONS

Here, again, are two subjects which make letter writing an enjoyable experience, and most of us will have to write such a letter at some time. I am always pleased to be able to wish friends "Good Luck" with their exams or when starting a new venture, or to be able to say "Congratulations" to them for some special achievement.

There are special cards which you can buy for these occasions and you could use one of these in which to write your note if you prefer.

LETTERS TO WISH "GOOD LUCK"

It is always nice to be able to wish someone "Good Luck", and there are many times when we can do just that. Some of the most usual ones follow.

New Job

One of the most frequent "Good Luck" letters is one to wish a colleague all the very best in a new job, and I begin by giving an example of this type of letter.

Dear Sarah,

I never really got a proper chance last night at your leaving celebrations to wish you the best of luck in your new job. We'll all miss you at Broxham's — life just won't be the same without you!

But less of my whingeing! I truly hope that this new job will give you every opportunity to progress in sales — an area which

I know you've not really been able to develop at Broxham's. From what you told me, it seems like just the right step for you, and I know you'll make a great success of it.

Do keep in touch and let me know how you're getting on. Maybe we could meet for a drink or lunch in a few weeks' time, when you're settled in? 'Til then ...

Love and very best wishes,

Friends Starting Their Own Business

With an increasing number of people now becoming self-employed, I thought it would be useful to include a letter of good luck to someone starting a new business. The following example is to a couple who have just set up their own small hotel.

Dear Roger and Vicki,

You made it! Well done! I just had to write and wish you every success with your new venture.

All the hard work must seem really worth it, now that you see what a beautiful place you've created for your guests. I remember coming over to you at Orchard Farm last Spring and thinking how brave you were embarking on such a task! All that renovation and conversion ...! (Do your guests know they're sleeping in what used to be the cow byre!?!)

I was pleased to hear that you've already got a lot of bookings, and I'm sure that once those people go back and tell all their friends what a good time they've had, your business will continue to go from strength to strength.

If you can find the time, do drop me a line in a few weeks to let me know how you're progressing.

All the very best,

Emigrating
There may be a time when you wish to write a good luck note to someone who is going abroad. My example letter is written to friends who are only going to be abroad for a couple of years; but it could easily be adapted for friends who are emigrating permanently.

Dear Jan,

Many thanks for your letter; Peter and I were so surprised to hear your news. It's wonderful that David's company is giving him the chance to work in the States for two years — what a marvellous opportunity for you both. But it's all happened so quickly; you can hardly know whether you're coming or going!

I think you're wise not to sell the house, and it's nice that you're letting it to someone you know.

What's your house like in New England? I hear it's a beautiful part of America, and I'm sure you'll love every minute of it.

By the time you get this letter you'll just about have your suitcases packed, and I'm sorry that it wasn't possible for us to travel down to say a personal "Goodbye". Peter and I just want to wish you and David all the very best of luck, enjoy yourselves, and please keep in touch.

With lots of love,

Entering A Competition
This could apply to many things: scout badges, ballet exams, beauty contests, fishing competitions, etc. The recipient of the following example letter is planning to enter his home-grown produce in the local country show and his niece is writing him a letter to wish him luck.

Dear Uncle Alan,

I was so sorry to have missed you when you called last night. Mum told me all about you entering your vegetables in next week's Uffcombe Show, and I just wanted to drop you a line to wish you good luck.

We all know how very hard you've worked in your garden this year, and if anyone deserves first prizes for everything − it's you!

I will be going to the Show, so will make a point of going straight to the Produce marquee to see how many rosettes and cups you've won! If you'll still be around at three o'clock, maybe you'd like to meet me at the tea tent for a celebration cuppa.

'Til then, we all wish you the very best of luck, and we're keeping our fingers crossed for you (not that you'll need it!).

With love and best wishes,

LETTERS TO SAY "CONGRATULATIONS"

There are many occasions when we like to give our friends a handwritten "pat-on-the-back", and some of the most common examples are given below.

Passing Exams

Dear Tracy,

Uncle Adrian and I were so pleased to hear that you passed your City & Guilds Hairdressing exams and that you've found a good job at a top London salon. You must be absolutely delighted. Our warmest congratulations to you.

Your mum tells me that after you've had a few years' work experience you hope to open your own salon. I think that's a wonderful idea; there's nothing like being your own boss. All the hard work and headaches are worth it, believe me!

Anyway, very well done, and hope to see you soon.

With our love and best wishes,

Job Promotion

Dear Richard,

I was delighted to hear about your promotion. Congratulations! I heard the news from Robert last night when we met for a game of squash.

You really do deserve this step up the ladder; I've often wondered when your company would recognise your talents, and now they have. Not before time, though!

This new direction will give you a lot of scope for developing your style, and I'm sure you'll soon be making your presence felt.

Well done − and all the very best.

Yours,

Driving Test Pass

Dear Pete,

Well done mate! I bumped into your sister in the High Street today, and she told me you passed your driving test the other week.

Have you got yourself a car yet? I know you had your eye on that little M.G. down at Green's Garage; will you be able to buy it now − or have you done so already?! If I know you, I'll bet you were straight down there, even before the ink had dried on your test pass certificate!

It's such a long time since I saw you. Let's get together soon

— maybe a trip down to the coast would be good for a laugh. We could go in my car and share the driving if you like? Let me know.

Well, congrats. again, and hope to see you soon.

All the best,

New Baby

Dear Laura,

Congratulations! Rob phoned us this morning with your wonderful news. A baby girl — you must be delighted; I know that you both secretly wanted a little girl.

Rob sounded absolutely ecstatic when he rang! He gave us the complete run-down of the proceedings and was so thrilled to have been involved at the actual birth. We were pleased to hear that you'd had not too difficult a time, and that you and little Zoe (love the name) are progressing well.

If it's O.K., we'll pop down to see you once you're settled back at home.

'Til then, take care of yourself — and Zoe!

With all our love and very best wishes,

16

SENDING AND REPLYING TO INVITATIONS

Invitations, particularly to parties, are becoming less and less formal, and often nowadays, people will make up their own funny invitation, or they may buy special invitation cards or pads; or they may phone. I personally think that just relying on the telephone is not such a good idea, as people are apt to forget the date. It is better if they have something in writing, and you may feel that a short note would be best. I have given below three example invitations for different occasions.

Invitation For Weekend Stay

Dear Mark and Angie,

Now that we have (at long last!) finished renovating our house, we wondered if you would like to come down and stay with us for a weekend next month. It's been so long since we've seen you, but as you know, it was just not possible for us to invite anyone when the house was in such a state.

It would be lovely to show you the area too. There are lots of delightful 'olde worlde' country pubs with real ale and home-cooked food, and there are several National Trust properties close by which we know you'd enjoy visiting.

We're busy the first weekend, but please drop us a line and let us know which of the other weekends would suit you, and we can take it from there.

Look forward to seeing you soon.

With our very best wishes,

Invitation To House-Warming Party

Dear *(name to be filled in by hand)*,

As you know, we have just had a very moving experience!

... and our new address is:

>   15, Herrington Crescent,
>   LONDON.
>   SW12 5TY
>   Tel: 071-600-0098

We're having a bit of a knees-up Saturday 14th March to celebrate
the move and to toast the new house, and would be delighted
if you could join us. We'll be kicking off at about 9.00 p.m. and
hope to see you then.

With best wishes,

Invitation To A Surprise Party

Dear *(name to be filled in by hand)*,

On 26th March, Philip will reach the ripe old age of 40!

To celebrate the fact, I'm arranging a **SURPRISE PARTY** for
him at The Doves Restaurant, Henley Street, Banbury, on 26th
March, and would love it if you could come along. There will
be a buffet supper and drinks laid on, as well as dance music.

If you are able to come, please can you arrive by 7.45 p.m. sharp, as I'll be arriving with Philip at about 8.00 p.m., and would like to have everyone there before us.

At the moment, Philip thinks that he and I are just going to the restaurant for a quiet candlelit dinner (won't he be disappointed!!) and I would really like to keep it that way − so if you see him please don't breathe a word.

Please let me know if you can come. I would be grateful if you could reply to the address above (which is our neighbour's address), as I obviously can't have any replies arriving at home!

Hope to see you on the 26th.

With best wishes,

To save you writing out several invitations, just do one (either typed or hand-written), have it photocopied, then fill in the names − it's much quicker!

REPLYING TO INFORMAL INVITATIONS

It is a very easy matter to reply to informal invitations, but I will give an example of an acceptance and a refusal which you may like to use as a guide.

Acceptance

Dear Carol,

Thank you so much for your kind invitation to the surprise party you are holding for Philip. We would be delighted to come. What a lovely idea; I can't wait to see his face when we all spring out of the woodwork!

As you know, Roger is seeing Philip for a round of golf on the same day, but don't worry; I have primed him not to mention it.

Look forward to seeing you at The Doves next month.

With our very best wishes and thanks,

Refusal

A letter of refusal is probably a little more difficult to write, as you do not want to offend anyone. If you have a previous engagement it is quite acceptable to refuse because of it, but I think it is courteous if you can say what the previous engagement is. All you need to do is write a short, simple, friendly letter, and leave it at that. An example could be:

Dear Mark and Sue,

Thank you so much for your invitation to the house-warming party, but I'm afraid we won't be able to make it as we have already made arrangements to spend the weekend with Caroline's sister in Dorset.

We'll be sorry to miss the party − your 'gatherings' are always such great fun! − but I hope that we can get together very soon. Hope you all have a good time on the 14th.

With our very best wishes and thanks,

FORMAL INVITATIONS

These are very useful when a large number of invitations need to be sent out. Also, for a more grand occasion − a wedding, for instance − a printed formal invitation undoubtedly looks better.

Cards can be purchased which are either specially printed or bought for the purpose at a stationer's. The quality of the invitation will obviously depend on how much you want to spend. Both the ready-bought ones and the specially printed cards will usually come with their own special envelopes.

A wedding is probably the most common occasion when a formal invitation card would be used, and I give below an example of the wording of such an invitation.

Mr. and Mrs. Dennis Clark
request the pleasure of the company of

. . . .

at the marriage of their daughter
Caroline Angela
with
Mr. Simon Charles Swinton
at St. Matthew's Parish Church
Harrington Road, Bath
on Saturday, 18th May, *year*
at 2.30 p.m.
and afterwards at
The Seagrove Hotel, Middle Street, Bath

3, Mere Close,
BATH,
Avon.
BA3 4HG   R.S.V.P.

Everyone knows R.S.V.P. means "Please Reply" and comes from the French phrase, "Repondez s'il vous plaît".

REPLYING TO FORMAL INVITATIONS

You should reply to such an invitation as soon as you receive it. There are special acceptance/refusal cards for wedding invitations, so you may prefer to send one of these instead of writing a letter. These are widely available from stationery shops.

If, however, you do want to send a note, it should be written on good quality notepaper. Make your answer as brief as possible, and, strictly speaking, it is correct to reply in the third person. A suitable formal reply to the above invitation would be:

Mr. and Mrs. Peter Mitchell thank Mr. and Mrs. Dennis Clark for their kind invitation to their daughter's wedding at St. Matthew's Church on Saturday, 18th May, *year*, and to a reception afterwards at The Seagrove Hotel, and are most happy to accept
(or, if you cannot attend)
regret that they will not be able to attend as they have accepted a previous engagement on that day.

This note should not be signed.

However, just because a formal invitation has been sent does not necessarily mean that you must send back a formal reply. Some people feel that a reply such as this is unnecessarily formal, especially if you know the people to whom you are writing. So you could write something like:

Dear Mr. and Mrs. Clark,

Thank you so much for your kind invitation to Caroline and Simon's wedding on Saturday, 18th May, and to the reception afterwards. Stuart and I would be delighted to attend and look forward to meeting you on that day.

Yours sincerely,

(sign your name in the usual way)

If you are unable to attend you could make the final sentence:

Unfortunately, Stuart and I will be on holiday that week, so we regret very much that we will be unable to attend.

Whichever style you choose, the main thing to remember is to be courteous and you will not go far wrong.

17

LOVE LETTERS

Perhaps in no field of letter writing are the opportunities for achievement greater. Between those who are in love, or between two people, one of whom is in love with the other, the letter can provide an opportunity for expression which would not be possible otherwise.

However, despite that, I would avoid being too passionate and 'flowery'. Although you might talk this way when you are together, I feel that such things are intensified when set down on paper. This is particularly so if you are writing to someone you do not know very well. In this cynical day and age, there is the danger that a passionate letter could appear grossly insincere, or even, in some unfortunate cases, be an object of ridicule. So be careful what you write. By all means let your loved one know you miss him (her), but don't be too elaborate about it; and do include other, more general, information in your letter which would be found interesting.

There is also one warning which might be worth noting about being too passionate in ink, and this is that there is always a danger of the letters getting into the hands of someone for whom they were not intended. One regularly sees this sort of thing being reported in the press as having happened to someone of note, and it is a sad fact that some unscrupulous people do have such a blatant disregard for the privacy of others. Don't think because you are just an ordinary person that it couldn't happen to you − it could; especially if you are involved in a risky or clandestine relationship.

You should always try to avoid writing and sending letters in the heat of the moment − either after a quarrel, or perhaps because you are a victim of unrequited love. At some later stage you may really regret having posted it. However, if you do write such a letter, keep it overnight and don't mail it until you have read it again the next day. If it is still appropriate, send it by all means, but you will most likely be glad that you didn't!

Another reason why you should choose your words carefully is that they could easily be misunderstood by the recipient — either by giving the impression that you are more interested than you really are; or by your not appearing to be interested enough.

There are many instances when you would write a letter to a loved one, and in the following I have tried to include some of the most common examples.

Married Couple — One Working Away From Home

It is not uncommon for lovers or married couples to be separated by hundreds of miles, and in these cases phoning every day may not be possible so they will have to keep in touch by post. These letters are fairly straightforward, and in a case where there is mutual understanding there should be no danger of anything written being misunderstood. These letters, therefore, can be long, and filled with material which will be interesting to the recipient.

My example letter comes from a wife whose husband is working away from home for a short while.

Dear Jon,

Well, here I am! Hope you're O.K. and having a good time — well not *too* good!

I went down to see my Mum and Dad on Saturday, and Mum and I spent a lovely day looking round all the shops — I didn't spend *too much* money! It was great; I managed to get all my Christmas shopping done. I can't believe how organised I am this year — you ought to go away just before Christmas *every* year! No, I didn't mean it!!

On Saturday evening I took Mum and Dad out for a bar meal to The Red Lion — you know, the little place at Cherringbury. The food was excellent. I stayed the night at my parents' rather than driving all the way back here.

I got home at about 10 o'clock on Sunday morning, and no sooner had I come through the door than *your* Mum phoned! She and your Dad popped over in the afternoon and ended up staying for dinner — we had a lovely time; it was nice to see them both.

So — what I thought was going to be a dismal weekend turned into a mad social whirl! I still missed you, though. I'd forgotten how lonely it can be — even when you're with family and friends.

I've been really busy at the office. That new project we've been working on is now in its final throes, so uncontrolled hysteria has broken out to get it finished on time. I've not been working too late though; in fact I've been getting home early enough to do a bit more decorating. I've finished painting all the woodwork in the hallway and dining room and I thought I'd do the hallway ceiling tonight if I've got time.

Oh, guess what? You remember I applied for tickets for us to see that new show in the West End? Well they arrived today and we've got fantastic seats — only two rows from the front. I can't wait!

You'll never guess what I've been roped into doing by our mad next door neighbours. I've said I'll go carol singing with them next week! I must have been asleep or something when I agreed to it! It should be a good laugh; about twenty of us are going round the town next Tuesday and Wednesday evenings; and it's all for a good cause — the church organ fund, I think. Peter and Julie have invited me to have a meal with them before we go out, so that'll be nice. Everyone's been really great — phoning and calling round to make sure I'm O.K. It's lovely of them to bother isn't it?

How are things with you? Hope your meetings are going well. Have you had chance to do any sightseeing yet? If so, what happened to my postcard?! I'm sure the next couple of weeks will go by quickly enough but it seems like an eternity 'til you come home. The old saying "Absence makes the heart grow fonder" is so true, but I could do without the "absence" to make me realise it.

Anyway, I'm writing this in my lunch break which is just about finished, so I'd better go and get back to the mass hysteria ...! If you have time, drop me a line and let me know how you're getting on. It really won't be long before you're back, so 'til then, take care.

All my love,

Holiday Romances
Quite often, people will meet on holiday and may wish to write to each other when they return home. Here again they may be separated by many miles, which always puts extra strain on any relationship. However, their correspondence could help the friendship develop, but they must be cautious about what they write, as one of them could easily get the wrong idea about the other's feelings.

The following example is written by a young man who has met a girl on holiday and whom he hopes to meet for dinner in a few weeks' time.

Dear Jackie,

Hope you arrived home safely and that the train journey wasn't too long and boring! It only took me half an hour to get back; after I'd found my car in the airport car park, that is! I spent ages looking for it and was beginning to think it had been stolen; but no, there it was, asleep in a quiet corner!

Although it's only been ten days since I got back, the holiday seems an age away. It's amazing how quickly you slip back into the old routine, isn't it? But it's nice to remember all the good times we had — all those lovely warm nights down at La Costa drinking gallons of sangria, then staggering back along the beach to the hotel ...

How's your work? Have you been busy? What have you been doing with yourself? Is there much to do up there; what sorts of places do you go out to? You must drop me a line and let me know how you're getting on.

Work has been keeping me very busy since I got back. We have an exhibition coming up at the end of next month, so I'm working hard putting all that together. It's my job to design the stand and make sure that all the things we want to take will fit on to it; and I'm pleased to say they do. It's looking really great − even though I do say so myself!

In fact, the exhibition is one of the reasons why I'm writing (apart from obviously wanting to find out how you are). By an amazing stroke of luck, the exhibition is being held in Manchester, and I will have to come up there for a few days when it is being assembled. As it's only about 20 miles away from where you are, I was wondering if we could meet for dinner or something while I'm up there?

I would really love to see you again, and hope that you'll be able to make time to meet me. I'll be in Manchester from the 20th of next month until the 25th. Let me know if any of those dates are good for you, then we can take it from there.

Look forward to hearing from you soon,

Girlfriend/Boyfriend At Different Universities

One of the most common forms of romantic separation is when one or both of a young couple goes away to college or university. These are especially difficult relationships to maintain because the two begin to make completely new lives for themselves and may end up growing apart. They will be meeting new people all the time, and will normally lead much more liberated and independent lives than when they lived at home. This can be very distressing if one drifts away but the other remains as romantically attached as before, and it is a sad fact that this type of relationship can often end in heartbreak.

The following example is written by a girl who has just moved away to one university and is writing to her boyfriend who has started at another.

Dear Tim,

Just thought I'd write you a quick letter to let you know how things are going here and to see how you're getting on.

I arrived at the halls of residence at about six o'clock on Saturday; my dad brought me down because I had a lot of stuff to bring. My room here is quite cosy and the halls are in a nice part of town. All the girls along my corridor are really friendly and have asked me to go out for a drink with them on Friday to the Union bar. There's a band on too, I think, so it should be quite good. Have you been out much? What are your digs like; is the landlady a "dragon"?

It's all so strange still − I've not really settled in properly yet. It's just so different from living at home. I really do miss you *so* much. When do you think you'll be able to come over for a visit? Try and come next weekend if you can. There's a good group on at the University, that you'd like.

Our lectures started today and all our tutors seem very pleasant. It's so nice − they actually treat you like adults − not like at school! We have quite a lot of work to do apart from the lectures, so I've made a point of disciplining myself to make sure I get all the work done. The university has a brilliant library where we can go and study, so I'm down there most days.

How's it all going with you? What's your course like, and the tutors, and the college − everything? Write and let me know how you're getting on. Have you made many friends yet − hope there aren't any attractive females there!

Anyway, I'd better go now. Lisa from next door has just popped her head round to see if I'm going down to dinner with her.

Write soon, won't you, and try to come down next weekend if you can.

Miss_you ...

All my love,

Breaking Off A Relationship
Unfortunately, there are times when writing a letter to a partner can be an extremely difficult matter. The most obvious occasion which springs to mind is when breaking off a relationship. Normally it is best to deal with this unpleasant and often emotionally painful situation face-to-face. However, some people feel that they can express their feelings better in writing, and prefer to send a letter to their partner for fear of being misunderstood if they discuss the matter in person.

The following example is a letter from a man who has been living with his fiancée, but has just walked out on her because he feels he cannot go through with the marriage.

Dear Jenny,

I realise that leaving like this and writing you a letter must seem like a total cop-out, but I just know I'd not be able to find the right words — or the courage — if you were here. I've no doubt that after you've read this you'll want to talk, and so do I, but I felt it would be easier — for both of us — if, first of all, I just took my things and went, and explained my reasons here in this letter.

The thing is, Jen, I just can't go through with the wedding. I've thought and thought about everything so much, and I've reached the agonising conclusion that our marriage just won't work. If we're honest with ourselves, the relationship's been on rocky ground for quite a while now, so what's it going to be like if we get married? It's so easy to let things just drift on and on, and I think one of our biggest faults has been the total lack of communication between us. Maybe we were hoping that by some miracle everything would just get better; but we can't sweep our problems under the carpet any longer.

Now that I've done this, I feel I must be totally blunt and honest with you. The plain fact is, Jen, that I'm really not in love with you enough to spend the rest of my life with you. For me, the problems began when we started living together; I just don't think we're well suited, either physically or emotionally, and there's no point in trying to make a situation work which is obviously not meant to be.

I just want you to know that there's no-one else, and never has been, and that it's breaking my heart having to do this to you. You're a really terrific person, and I hope there will be some way in which we can still be friends after this awful time in our lives has passed.

I will be staying at my brother's for a while and will be there if you want to call me.

Talk to you soon,

(The writer of this letter would probably then just sign his name. Neither "Love" nor "Best wishes" as a closing line would really be appropriate.)

18

BAD NEWS, APOLOGIES, AND GET WELL MESSAGES

BAD NEWS

Being the bearer of bad tidings is never an easy task, but it is often less distressing to put unfortunate news in a letter than it is to tell it to people face-to-face.

News Of An Impending Divorce

The first example letter deals with the unhappy situation where a wife is writing to a friend to say that her husband has asked her for a divorce.

Dear Rachel,

Rather than you hearing my unhappy news second-hand, I want you to know that after thirty four years of marriage my beloved Jeremy has asked me for a divorce in order to marry his mistress. Under the unpleasant circumstances I have had to agree; this has caused both me and the children deep distress.

At present my future is very uncertain; however, I am living at the above address until the end of February. I hope that you will keep in touch as I have always valued your friendship.

Yours,

Child Killed In An Accident

The next example of a "bad news" letter is where a father is writing to friends to say that his daughter has been killed in a road accident. News of this nature would be particularly distressing to convey in person and I would imagine that people would find it much easier to write.

Dear Andrew and Margaret,

I am so sorry to have to write to you like this but I just couldn't find the courage to telephone you with our devastating news.

I'm afraid that Joyce and I will have to cancel our stay with you next weekend, as Janice was killed in a road accident on Saturday evening. You may have seen the reports about the pile-up in fog on the M25; well Janice was one of the drivers involved.

As you can imagine, Joyce and I are absolutely distraught, but we are fortunate that Mike and Sarah have been able to get back here, now, as we all share the worst of our grief.

The funeral is being held on Friday and after that we will be trying to pick up the pieces and get on with life. If I may, I will be in touch in a little while to arrange another visit which I'm sure, then, will be just what we need.

With our best wishes to you both.

Yours,

APOLOGIES

Here again, people may find it is easier to send a note of apology than to say a personal "sorry" to someone they have offended. I have given three examples of apology letters which cover quite different subjects.

Speaking Out of Turn

Dear Eleanor,

I realise that I'm probably the last person you would expect (or want) to get a letter from, but I have been so worried about yesterday that I just had to write to you.

The first and most important thing I want to say is "Sorry". I can't think what possessed me to be so rude and thoughtless. My only excuse (and it's a pretty pathetic one!) is that I was having a really bad day yesterday, and when you called with your problem it was just the straw that broke the proverbial camel's back and I just lashed out. But that is no excuse, and my behaviour was totally unacceptable and uncalled for, and completely unforgiveable.

I know I should have thought of it yesterday before I opened my big mouth, but I really would be very sorry if this incident totally ruined our friendship — even though you would be perfectly justified in never speaking to me again. I don't want to go on and on, but I just really hope that you will be able to accept my apology.

Please call me if you feel you can.

With my sincerest best wishes,

Accidentally Hurting Someone's Dog
The next letter is one to someone whom the writer does not know and deals with an accident involving the stranger's dog.

Dear Mr. Jackson,

I just wanted to write and say how sorry I am for knocking your dog, Tara, over yesterday. I know you have taken her to the vet and that the injury to her leg is not serious, but I still feel absolutely dreadful.

You have been so good about the whole thing, and I know that there was nothing I could have done to avoid the accident. But, having a dog of my own, I can appreciate how upsetting it is when something like this happens.

I'm so glad Tara will be O.K., and although you said yesterday that you wouldn't dream of letting me give you anything towards her vet's bill, I feel it is the least I can do, so I would be very pleased if you would accept the enclosed cheque which should at least cover some of the cost.

Thanks again for being so understanding, and I hope Tara makes a full recovery very soon.

With my best wishes,

Unable to Keep An Appointment
If you are unable to keep an appointment, for whatever reason, it is always a nice idea to write a short note of apology, as in the next example.

Dear Katherine,

I just wanted to write you a quick note to apologise for not being able to keep our theatre date last night.

It's just typical, isn't it! We book up weeks and weeks in advance and what happens − I go and get the 'flu and miss what was, I'm sure, a truly unforgettable evening.

I was so relieved you managed to get Michelle to go with you at such short notice; I would never have forgiven myself if you had gone on your own, or missed it altogether. Did she enjoy the show? Please give me a call when you have a minute, and tell me all about it.

With love and best wishes,

GET WELL MESSAGES
One is always concerned when learning that a friend or relative is unwell, so it is nice to be able to send them a get well greeting. There are special cards for this purpose which can be bought

from most stationery shops. You could buy one of these cards and write a little note inside; however, it would be just as much appreciated if you wrote a letter on a good sheet of notepaper.

Below are some different examples of "Get Well" messages.

"Get Well" Message To A Friend
The following letter is a straightforward message to a friend to say "Get Well".

Dear Alison,

I saw David in town today and he told me you're laid up with a bad back. How awful for you. A slipped disc is such a painful thing; I remember when I had one a couple of years ago, I was in agony. Has the doctor said how long you'll be out of action?

I just wanted to say "Get Well Soon" and I hope that this little card will cheer you up a bit. Maybe I could pop over for a cup of tea and a natter one evening? I'll call in a day or two to see when would be a good time.

Hope you'll soon be feeling much better.

Lots of love,

Sending "Get Well" Greetings Via Someone Else
A variation of a "Get Well" message is writing to the partner or relative of someone who is ill so that they can pass on greetings for you.

Dear Mary,

I was so sorry to hear that Denis has been taken into hospital, and I just wanted to write this little note to ask you to pass on our best wishes to him for a speedy recovery.

If you need a lift up to the hospital or into town, Gordon and I will be only too pleased to help, and if there's anything at all that you need you only have to ask.

Once again, our fondest get well greetings to Denis for a speedy recovery, and our very best wishes to you.

Love,

19

LETTERS OF SYMPATHY

These are probably the most difficult of all letters that you will ever have to write; although there are some people who have a gift for them.

In past years, when writing letters of condolence following a bereavement, it was customary to write a lengthy letter dealing with certain aspects of the deceased's life and perhaps mentioning such matters as his long association with this or that, but generally the message of sympathy is apt to be lost in words describing matters which are usually very obvious to the recipient, and therefore unnecessary. In such instances, a simple sincere message usually meets the case best.

Even if you are well acquainted with the person to whom you are writing, it is always difficult to convey true sincerity without sounding gloomy or dramatic. My advice would be to keep sympathy letters fairly short and not try to write too much. Care is also necessary in case any double meaning is accidentally conveyed, and it is also very easy to sound extremely tactless in these letters − so beware! One thing to remember is that there is usually something positive in any unfortunate situation, and it is a good idea to try and be as optimistic as possible when writing letters of sympathy.

Although bereavement is the most obvious occasion when you would write a sympathy letter, it is by no means the only one. Many instances require a letter of this kind − from a house fire to exam failure.

However, as bereavement is the most common, I will deal with this first, and the following examples cover a variety of different condolence letters. In the first three, the letter writers are assumed to be quite good friends of the people to whom they are writing; the fourth is from someone who is only an acquaintance.

Parent Died

Dear Jane,

I was so sorry to hear the sad news about your Mum. It seems like only yesterday that you and I were coming in from school and she was giving us cheese on toast and those delicious home-made cakes.

She was always so good to me, and I will really miss her. I can only begin to imagine what a terrible time this must be for you and your family. I will, of course, be coming (*to the funeral*) on Friday and will see you then, but if you need *anything* in the meantime, please don't hesitate to call, will you?

Please send my condolences to your Dad and to Neil.

Love,

Child Died

Dear Sue and Steve,

I saw Eileen today who told me of your dreadful loss, and I just wanted you both to know that Vicki and I are thinking of you all at this terrible time. How is little Sarah taking it? It must be a comfort having her there with you.

I realise that at this moment you must be feeling utterly wretched, but I hope it may help you to know that the same thing happened to my sister, Helen, three years ago, when she lost her little boy through cot death. After her heartbreaking experience she started up a support group for parents like yourselves, and she has given hope and comfort to a great many people over the last couple of years. I know it's still early days yet, but if you feel you would like to give her a call, either now or in the future, I know she would be pleased to hear from you. Her number is Stubbington 8996875.

I do hope this may be of some help and that we will see you soon under happier circumstances.

With our love and best wishes,

Baby Stillborn

Dear Janet,

I met Peter in the supermarket tonight and he broke your sad news to me. I'm sure I can't even pretend to know how devastated you must feel, but I was relieved to learn that the doctors say you will have no long-lasting physical effects and that it was a chance in a million that this tragedy happened. Even so, that must seem like small comfort at the moment.

Peter says you are coping well, and if I know you, I'm sure that's true. With your down-to-earth approach to life and your strength and determination, I know you'll be able to put this unhappy time behind you.

If you'd like me to call round for an evening I'd love to come, but if you'd rather not, I understand perfectly. Just let me know.

With all my love and best wishes,

Husband Died Tragically

Dear Mrs. McLeod,

I was stunned to read the report in today's local paper of Alan's dreadful accident. How awful for you to lose him so tragically. The suddenness of such a loss is particularly upsetting, and the unfairness of losing one so young can never be fully understood.

My husband, John, and I just wanted you to know that our thoughts are with you and the family at this sad time. Alan was always such a cheerful person and so helpful when he called, and I know he will be sorely missed by many people in the town.

We do hope you will be able to find the courage to pick up the pieces and carry on, and we wish you everything that is good for the future.

With our kindest regards.

Yours sincerely,

The following are examples of sympathy letters for all kinds of occasions.

Exam Failure

Dear Graham,

I was sorry to hear from your Mum that you won't be going to medical school next year. You must be so disappointed; Uncle Alan and I know how much becoming a doctor has always meant to you.

Your Mum tells me you will try again next year and that you have got a job, in the meantime, at the local hospital. I know you will enjoy it, and it'll be very good experience for you. You never know, in a few years' time you might be glad you didn't get into medical school this term!

Both Uncle Alan and I wish you every happiness in your new job, and every success when you take your exams again.

I do hope we'll see you in the not-too-distant future.

With all our love,

Failed Business

Dear Jeff,

I was so sorry to hear that your business venture didn't work out, and after all the hard work and effort you put in, too. What a blow. If anybody deserved to succeed, you did. It was just your luck that as soon as you started trading the lending rates went sky-high and the economy headed for a recession. So many small businesses are going the same way, and it's a tragedy to see all the hope and optimism turn into misery and despair. Anyway, at least you can say you "had a go" which is more than most of us can.

But I just know you'll bounce back from this, and I hear that you're already fixed up with a job; I hope all goes well.

Look forward to seeing you soon.

With my very best wishes,

House Fire

Dear Terry and Jean,

We were very sorry to hear about the fire; what a terrible thing to happen to you so soon after setting up home.

I am also writing to let you know that we have a spare bed and a dining suite stored away doing nothing in our loft, and we would be delighted to lend them to you 'til you get sorted out. They're not great to look at, but will do the job until you can get something more suitable.

If you are O.K. and don't need these, don't bother to get in touch as I know you will have a lot on your minds at present. But please don't hesitate to give us a call if you'd like the furniture; it would be no trouble to drop it round.

Hope things are soon looking brighter for you.

With very best wishes,

Burglary

Dear Ted,

We were so sorry to hear the terrible news that you had a break-in last week. It must have been dreadful to come back and find the house in such a state. At least they didn't take anything of sentimental value − I suppose that's something. Is Betsy still very upset? Having a burglary is one of Christine's biggest dreads. It's such an awful thing I just don't think she could cope if it happened to us.

The positive thing you mentioned in your letter is the fact that the police seem to have a good idea who is responsible. Have they managed to catch him yet?

I do hope that you will both be able to put this terrible incident behind you. Now that you have made your house more secure, I'm sure you must feel a lot happier.

Please give our love to Betsy, and we hope to see you both very soon.

With best wishes,

Made Redundant

Dear Sam,

It was nice to see you again today, but I was very sorry to learn that your company has been taken over and that you have been made redundant. It must be very sad for you after all these years; I know how much you enjoyed your job. You'd think that if you worked for a company for as long as you have they'd show a bit more respect; to be given just three days' notice is a disgrace. I suppose the one good thing is that at least your redundancy payment should be quite good.

So, what will you do now? Have you any plans? It would be nice to hear what you have in mind; I didn't really get a chance to chat about it today. Maybe it's time you and Betty moved down to the coast and started that little guest house you've always dreamed about? In a few years' time you'll probably look back and see this redundancy as a godsend!

Do keep in touch, won't you, and let me know how you're doing.

All the very best to you and to Betty,

INDEX

FREE

If you would like an up-to-date list of all **RIGHT WAY** titles currently available, please send a stamped self-addressed envelope to

ELLIOT RIGHT WAY BOOKS,
KINGSWOOD, SURREY, KT2O 6TD, U.K.
or visit our web site at www.right-way.co.uk